# reliable roses

Philip Harkness

*Photography by Steve Wooster*

COLLINS & BROWN

First published in Great Britain in 2004
by Collins & Brown Limited
The Chrysalis Building
Bramley Road
London W10 6SP

An imprint of Chrysalis Books Group plc



9 8 7 6 5 4 3 2 1

British Library Cataloguing-in-Publication Data: A catalogue record for this book is available from the British Library.

ISBN: 1-84340-114-2

Designed by Gemma Wilson
Edited by Sharon Amos
Indexed by Michele Clarke
Proofread by Lydia Darbyshire

Color reproduction by Classic Scan, Singapore
Printed in China by Imago

# Contents

# Introduction

Roses are wonderful plants that nature has endowed with many beautiful features. In this book I aim to explore ways of enjoying roses and to investigate the best ways of achieving good results without spending too much time in the garden. My approach is based on the fact that there are two important aspects to growing and enjoying roses.

First, roses are planted in the garden for recreation, interest and pleasure. We should not be ashamed that our pursuit is hedonistic.

Second, to make our rose growing successful we should, wherever possible, try to work with nature and never against it.

In practical terms, this book is designed to make growing roses easier and more enjoyable. It will help you to use the characteristics that nature provides to reduce problems in the cultivation of plants. It will not be a technical tour de force, laden with history, science, genetics or botanical classification. There will be no in-depth discussion on the pathological make-up of the plant nor on the implications of applying chemicals. Our aim is to derive the greatest possible pleasure from this group of plants, using their natural beauty and enhancing it in whatever ways we can.

In this book there is a selection of cultivars that you may wish to grow in your garden. The choice of a good rose is a subjective matter. If it provides the features that you deem to be important in a way that gives you pleasure, it is a good rose for you, and that is all that is important. There is a mixture of cultivars, some old and some new, but all have good qualities. Few roses have no faults, but I hope that this selection will introduce you to the vast range of different shapes and forms that are available to the modern gardener.

Our introduction to this adventure is to look at the diversity of the rose genus. What nature began, man has improved upon, developing further the rose's beautiful features. Today we are able to enjoy the rose in a myriad different forms.

*Left: The rose is extremely versatile and can be used in mixed plantings, cottage gardens or formal settings and to cover structures.*

*Above: Make a feature of a rose by allowing it to climb over an area or pergola.*

The genus family includes plants that grow happily as miniatures, never more than 30–38cm (12–15 in) tall: these are neat compact plants, miniature in leaf, flower and bush. At the other extreme there are rampant climbing and rambling roses. It is not unusual to find plants capable of growing to more than 10m (30 ft) tall. In between, there are roses that make perfect garden plants – there is something suitable for every garden and for every taste.

With such an overawhelming choice of size, style and type it is hard to know where to start. There is a niche in every garden for a climbing or rambling rose. Watch it cover a fence, building or pergola or enjoy the spectacular effect of a rose flowering high in a tree. Those roses categorized as ground cover are just as easy to place in the garden to prevent the influx of weeds and provide colour and, best of all, they are easy to maintain.

Then there are patio and border cultivars. Growing taller than miniatures, but smaller than bush roses, they are always worth a try in tubs, planters and in borders.

Going up in size we then come to the largest type, bush roses. These are subdivided into hybrid tea (large-flowered), floribunda (cluster-flowered) and grandiflora (taller, usually with clusters of flowers). All are great garden plants. They flower for a long time, repeat flowering through summer and somtimes into early winter. They can range from 1m (3ft) tall to at least 1.8m (6ft) tall. There are only two questions to ask when you are buying: Do I like them? Where will they go in my garden? Beyond that, there is no logical reason to have a prejudice against any particular rose. If you answer the first question with a 'yes', then it is irrelevant whether it is classified as a hybrid tea or floribunda. It is only blinkered dogma that allows you to say, 'Yes I like it', only to discover that it is a floribunda and say, 'I don't like it, as I don't like floribundas.' Have an open mind and do not let irrelevant classifications and labels cloud your judgement.

The final group are shrub roses. This term covers all that are left. Many are modern cultivars, others old and some ancient, the species from which all modern roses have evolved. Most of them will grow bigger and wider than bush roses – 1.8–4m (6–12ft) tall and sometimes up to 2.4m (8 ft) wide. Needless to say, there are many shrub roses that are smaller than these dimensions so always carefully check the mature height before purchasing. The other point to bear in mind is that the older shrub roses will flower only once in summer, while most of the modern roses will repeat bloom.



These descriptions of the most basic forms, only touch the surface of how individual roses may grow. Within each category there will be flowers of all different shapes and sizes. A rose can produce a flower with a minimum of five petals (known as a single flower) or it may have 10–15 petals (a semi-double flower). At the other extreme there may be up to 100 petals in one flower. To fall in with convention, although it is not very helpful, those with 20 petals and more are referred to as double flowers, so one term covers a wide range of blooms. Flowers can be less than 2.5cm (1in) across to more than 13cm (5in ) across. There are so many permutations that there is always a rose somewhere to appeal to every person.

But this is only touching on the look of the flower. There is the magic that chemistry cannot copy: the range of satisfying rose perfumes. Our noses can have as much pleasure as our eyes. Perfumes range from light to heady, from sweet to spicy; there may be hints of apple, honey, citronella or many more.

As we get to know the rose, we will understand that it is a hardy and resilient garden plant. Roses withstand a vast range of ambient and climatic conditions. Some thrive in shady positions, while other prefer the sun; all will grow in positions with moderate or above average sunlight. Some roses are winter hardy to temperatures of –10°C (14°F), but others will

*Below: Roses can extend the flowering season of mixed plantings and add glorious perfume.*

*Right: Roses are some of the most beautiful climbing plants and look wonderful over an arch.*

suffer in frost. All will withstand lower winter temperatures if they are protected from cold winds. In this book zones are used to indicate hardiness, and these refer to regions on the North American continent.

This book is written in the hope that it will encourage a love and appreciation of the rose and that it will act as a guide to help dispel myths, explain intricacies but, most of all, show how easy it is to grow and enjoy roses.

# Easy Road to Perfect Roses

# Nature's Elements

This chapter title is misleading. There are some aspects of growing roses in which there are no short cuts and the only way to achieve good results is by old-fashioned hard work. The trick is to assess the strengths that nature has provided and to utilize them.

The first requirement is to define our personal goals. We all want the best results possible, but we must put the term 'best results' into our personal context, and every gardener will have a different answer. Are you looking for perfection, with no damage from insects or disease? Do you tolerate some imperfections, not getting too worried over an insect attack or low-level disease? Do you manage your garden in a wholly organic, natural way, without artificial chemicals of any sort? Whatever answers you gave to these questions, some of the ideas here will help you increase the pleasure your roses give to you. In a garden the elements supplied by nature are sun, wind, rain, soil, frost and time. With care and management they can be used to benefit roses.

## Sun

The positive purpose of the sun is to provide the energy source for the plant to manufacture food from the nutrients and water it extracts from the soil. In theory, all roses need sunlight for this process. In practice, there are some roses that will grow in areas with very little direct sunlight, although the site must still be light.

The intensity of sunlight is largely a function of latitude: the nearer you are to the equator, the more intense the sunlight. As you move away from the equator the intensity of the sunlight is less, but the hours of sunlight increase during the summer, so that what is lost in intensity is partially recovered in longer hours. Hot, intense sunlight can have a detrimental effect. On some cultivars it will cause scorching of young foliage or even of the flowers (darker colours are more

*Below: Roses excel in a more formal planting schemes creating stunning impact with blocks of colour.*

prone to this because they absorb more heat). Think about your local climate, and in areas with intense sunlight plan to give the roses a little shade in the middle of the day to protect them from the hottest sun. In cooler regions try to plant where the rose can benefit from longer hours of sunlight. Doing this will give the rose the best chance to please you.

## Wind

Different types of wind will affect the way your roses grow. We will divide them into summer and winter winds.

### SUMMER WINDS

Most places have a prevailing wind, either warm or cold. Warm summer winds will not cause a lot of damage to roses. The exception to this is in hot areas, where hot, dry winds will dehydrate plants. Counteract this by planting in the lee of the wind and by providing irrigation. If the summer wind is cold this can cause more problems, the worst of which is encouraging some diseases by providing an environment in which there can be large, rapid fluctuations in temperature. Downy mildew thrives in these conditions. The remedy lies in your choice of resistant varieties and in selecting a site that offers protection from the worst of the prevailing winds. A cold summer wind in cooler and more exposed regions may also mean the overall height of the plant will be reduced if there is a regular strong, cold wind.

Both summer and winter winds can cause physical damage. As the rose stems, known as canes, wave in the wind, they will rub together, causing abrasions. These are no different from a cut or graze on your arm. An open wound provides easy access to bacteria or disease, so in sites that are regularly exposed to strong winds, shorter plants will do better than taller ones.

### WINTER WINDS

Winter winds can also cause physical damage. Soil is often moist in the winter, and if the plant is tall, a strong wind will rock it in the soil, making the roots loose and reducing their ability to feed the plant. The solution is simple: give the plant an early winter prune to reduce the area that can catch the wind.

In cold areas winter winds can be very damaging. When the plant is not protected from winter wind it will suffer from the colder temperature caused by the wind-chill factor, which can freeze the fluids in the stem, rupturing the vessels that carry food and water. These will not repair themselves, so the damage is permanent. It is essential to choose hardy varieties and to protect them from cold winds.

## Rain

Roses like plenty of moisture – without water there is no life. If you are in a dry area, you must supply water to make up for the lack of natural rainfall. Watering is best done in the morning. If it takes place in the evening the area around the rose can remain humid overnight and encourage the onset of downy mildew. In an area where you have to water because it is hot and there is not enough natural rainfall, plants will often grow taller than normal – if you supply enough water. Too much rain in a soil that retains moisture means that damage from excess rain

*Right: Some roses suffer damage from rain, when the petals may be bruised and in some cases the flower may never open.*

occurs if the roses stand in waterlogged soil. The roots will begin to rot and die. Either plant elsewhere or improve the drainage.

## Soil

The soil in which it is planted is vital to a rose. It has the same importance as the foundation has to a building. Without good soil to support growth you can't have a top-quality plant.

Roses like good, fertile soil with lots of decayed organic material in the form of well-rotted farmyard manure or composted vegetation. They like plenty of moisture but not to stand in water. Adding organic material will help roses in any soil. In light, free-draining soils, adding organic material retains more water. In heavy, wet soils, adding this material improves drainage.

Roses are highly adaptable. They thrive in a wide range of different soils. Check the pH of your soil. Add lime to increase the pH (alkaline value) of very acid soil. Adding organic material will help to reduce the pH value of very alkaline soil. You may need to add iron in the form of soluble chelated iron to alkaline soils so that the plants can take up all the nutrients they need.



There is no substitute for working the soil before planting. The rose will want to develop a deep root system, and its roots need to penetrate the soil easily. Dig the soil well: the deeper you dig the better – but don't bury yourself. Remember that the soil is the foundation to hold the plant up and the larder to store all its food. The only time you can make improvements to the soil is before you plant. Digging the soil well improves the structure, allowing easier penetration for the roots. Adding compost, manure or other plant foods will stock up its reserves of food, giving the rose a better start in life.

## Frost

There are three different stages in a plant's annual cycle when frost can have a damaging effect.

Plants that were pruned in early spring will have produced fast-growing, lush, red shoots. These are full of moisture and potential and may be anything from 5–25cm (2–10 in) long. These shoots are very vulnerable to frost damage. The very moisture that will promote rapid growth may also prove to be their downfall. If a spring frost is severe enough to freeze young shoots, they will never fully recover. The moisture turns to ice, and, as it does so, it expands, bursting the vessels that carry the moisture. Those tubes will never again carry food or water for the plant.

A frost might damage only 10 per cent of the tubes in the stem, or it may damage 80 per cent. After light damage the stem will continue to grow until one day the plant needs all the food and water it can muster. The day that the flowers open puts maximum demand on the supply of food and water, and suddenly there is a shortage. And the flowers wither and die without ever showing us their beauty.

If the damage was more severe the whole stem may wither away without warning on a hot summer day. The damaged stem can never recover; it will only become weaker. Supporting a weak stem is like having a parasite – it takes nutrients from the plant but does not contribute.

After a spring frost you need to be able to recognize the extent of the damage. The general guide is that if all the leaves at the top of the stem go limp and hang forlornly, the damage is serious and you should cut the stem back to allow another unaffected stem to grow and replace it. The other visual effect is when the edges and tips of the leaves discolour, eventually turning brown and crispy. This usually means that just the edges of the leaves have suffered and this will not cause any long-term problems. The best remedial action is to acknowledge that you are in an area that has late spring frost, and adjust the timing of your spring pruning accordingly. If you prune later in the year the plants may be less susceptible to this type of damage. Try to avoid getting swept into the mind set that modern consumerism and retailing promote: that 'now' or 'early' is best. Instead, think of nature's calendar and work in a natural time frame, not one to suit commercial interests.

### AUTUMN FROSTS

A sudden autumn frost can cause damage, especially when the plant is still in bloom and there is plenty of movement of fluids to support the flowers. The presence of these fluids makes the plant vulnerable. In the same way as young shoots can be damaged by a late spring frost, so a sudden autumn frost will affect flowering stems. Just how badly will become visible when pruning the following spring: the pith in the centre of the stem will be coloured brown and must be cut out. A stem like this will never prosper and you will be better off without it.

WINTER FROSTS

Roses are able to withstand much colder temperatures while they are dormant, because the amount of fluid in the stems is reduced and the effect of freezing is reduced. The combination of frost and biting wind is more damaging than cold temperatures on their own. Protection from wind and cold can be given with netting, straw or other insulating materials.

## Time

Time is the commitment we make to a garden. Roses can be made to perform well without becoming a burden, but remember that there are some tasks – soil preparation before planting, pruning in spring, for example – that must be done before we can relax in summer and enjoy the fruits of our labour. Don't expect something for nothing. If you put in the minimum effort, the results will be reasonable but not perfect.

It is rare to have all the natural elements in perfect balance. The trick is to know that where one aspect is weak, so we be fair to the plant and give it the best chance by providing good conditions in other areas. There will always be a compromise, and that is acceptable as long as it is a fair compromise. It is only when there are too many poor resources that the plant will refuse to behave as we want it to. Unless we provide a nurturing environment and a solid foundation our plants can never fulfil their potential.

*Below: The effect may be pretty, but any soft young growth will be damaged by an unexpected frost.*

# Planning and Design

Here we enter one of the most enjoyable areas of gardening. This is our chance to create our own landscape in harmony with nature. You can employ a professional designer, who may provide a wonderful garden design. The alternative is to allow your garden to evolve organically. As you change the garden over the years and as you incorporate different features, the plants and ideas you have will be your own. These ideas will be a reminder of a phase of your life, of a person or a place you visited. A garden is a living entity, developing and evolving all the time. No design is ever complete: there are always changes you can make to include some new feeling from your life.

Roses can be incorporated in any and every garden. They are just like you and your clothes. Sometimes you go to work in a suit, to give the right impression. On many occasions you are at leisure in shorts and a T-shirt. In the evening you might wear evening dress to create an elegant, graceful air. There is a time and place for each style. Roses are the same. They can be functional, graceful or beautiful; they are certainly versatile and able to blend into formal or informal designs. Some appear to be bashful and shy; others are bold and brash. All have a beauty for us to discover and enjoy. A garden is a place to reflect moods: the rose helps to create these effects.



The first task in design is to select a position that will suit the plants. We have already looked at the factors that will influence how plants perform – they need a light position with some direct sunlight, but they do not want to be overshadowed by trees. As a guide, assume that the roots of a mature tree will affect the soil in the entire area under the canopy and for another 3m (10 ft) beyond. It is not just the light that is compromised by the tree: it takes moisture and food from the soil as well. Good fertile soil is required, which is not too wet and not too dry. Think about the wind, the frost and other natural aspects. Take this opportunity to design trouble out of your garden.

The second task is to decide what size plants you want to grow. This is important and should be done before you start thinking whether you want red, pink or any other colour. The ultimate size of the plant will dictate whether it is the right rose for the position you have selected. It is virtually impossible to reduce the size of a rose plant. If, with careful pruning the plant grows to 1.2m (4 ft) tall, then that is its size. It is possible

*Below: Use a rampant climber or rambler to cover a building. The effect is informal but effective.*

*Above: The colours in this informal planting blend beautifully together.*

to let it grow taller with lighter pruning, but it is not possible to reduce the size without some undesirable side effects, such as constant summer pruning, which will reduce the amount of bloom the plant can produce.

Ascertaining the size of a plant can be difficult. Different books and catalogues often assign a rose with a range of ultimate heights. To plan the garden we need to understand how nurserymen accredit the heights to cultivars, and how our garden's microclimate and growing conditions will affect height. Remember that it is best to work with nature.

As a rule, nurserymen will give the minimum height that you can expect a rose cultivar to attain. This is a logical starting point, given the fundamental rule that you can let it get taller. Factors that will influence the size of the plant in your garden are:

**Soil** A rich, fertile soil will grow a stronger and taller plant. A light, poor soil will grow a weaker and smaller plant.

**Sun** In a region that is sunny with warmer weather early in the year, more growth will be produced (provided there is enough water), giving a bigger plant.

**Wind** In a windy position the plant will react by remaining shorter, especially in cold wind.

**Rain** Without enough water in the growing season the plant will remain smaller. With a combination of sun, heat and water all together, the plant will become larger.



*Below: An example of a rough planting plan. The plants in the front will all be slightly shorter than those behind them, and the colours are arranged in a symmetrical pattern from left to right and viewed from either end or from the front.*

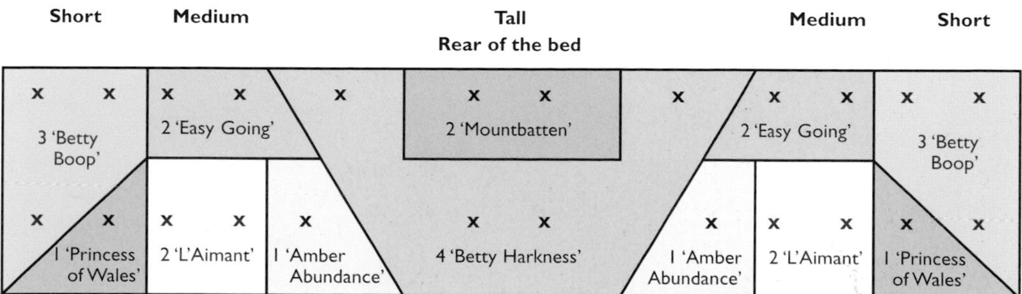

*Above: The formal walkway is a visual treat as well as enthralling for the sense of smell.*



## Dimensions

The third task is to walk into the garden and plan the area that we want to plant. It is two dimensional on the ground but we have to also consider for the third dimension – the height of the plants. We can get shape into our rose garden by adjusting the length and breadth of the area we are planting. We can have an area that is any shape, a square, rectangle, circle or random curves. We can also get shape into our garden by using the different heights of the plants. Effects can be introduced, such as undulations to give the impression of waves, or graduating from shortest to tallest or introducing sudden peaks of height.

The fourth task is to jot down a rough plan on paper. It need not be to scale, but it should include the following information. Note the rough shape of the area, and add the dimensions. It always helps to show where north is, because then you can assess the light, sunrise and sunset. Next, draw in any prominent features: big trees that will affect light and soil; paths; your house; eyesores that you want to block out; any slope to the site. Add a couple of arrows showing your prime viewing directions. How will it look from the patio, window, entrance gate? Do I need a tall plant to block a view of the compost area?

## Choosing a Style

The fifth task is to decide what style you want reflected in the garden. Some roses are light, airy, graceful and elegant. Others are strong, bold and almost heavy. Do you want a definite statement, using an intense splash of colour, or a subtle complement to other aspects of the garden? Are you mixing colours or planting in groups of the same cultivar? There are many questions of style, fashion and individual choice. The last is the important one: remember who the garden is for and who it should please most. Do it in your own way and enjoy your own interaction with nature.

## Preparing a Planting Plan

Task six is to start thinking about a planting plan. By now you know the shape and size of the area for planting, the size of the plants and the style you wish to express. The only remaining jobs are the planting plan and the colours. To draw a planting plan you need to use an accurate scale. Decide on the planting distance that you want to use – 75cm (30in) apart is a good average – and mark the planting positions on the plan. Either plant in rows, or in staggered rows.

Make a list of those cultivars you want to include, the 'must have' list. The second list is 'I like it but I can live without it'. If you are planting in groups now is the time to divide up the plants. Three of a kind is usually the minimum; five give a dash of colour; seven and more give a splash of colour. Try to use groups of different sizes. If all the roses are planted in the same number – all threes or all fives – they will look regimented and lack vitality and inspiration.

It is always a good policy to select the tallest roses first. The main reason for this is that are fewer taller varieties than shorter ones, so it is wise to build the design around the available taller cultivars. It is now a process of personal choice. Selecting colours that contrast or graduate gently in tone is one way. Alternatively consider a random use of colour, or use colours within one range – say pinks and reds, or oranges to yellows. Or use the colours to create symmetry or a pattern. Find pictures of the roses you like and place cut-outs on your plan to give an idea of the colour selections you have made.

Some traditionalists argue that roses should be grown alone. I disagree. My suggestion is that roses are unusual as garden plants in that they make a wonderful display on their own. There are very few species that have the array of attributes found in every rose garden, but because it is possible to create successful gardens from roses alone, the rose has suffered from an ill-informed view that it is a loner and that it only likes its own company. How wrong that is. It is a great mixer. It can add colour, shape or perfume to a multitude of garden styles. Climbing roses can be grown in tandem with clematis, increasing both the flowering time and the colour range available. Mixed shrub borders benefit from the intensity of a flowering rose, the perfume and flowering time. Ground cover roses provide brilliant displays in patio tubs and in hanging baskets. There is no position that is forbidden if you keep an open mind.

*Right: Many cities have excellent public rose gardens which are ideal places to see a range of cultivars.*

# How to Choose

Knowing how to choose the plants you want will make everything easier. In some respects it is like decorating your home. In the kitchen you will be looking for colours that suit the activities and a floor covering that will withstand wear and tear. A bedroom will require a different approach: there may be softer colours, there may be lace, there may be more romance.

## New or old cultivars

Both new and old cultivars can be beautiful. There are good new roses and others that are not so good. The same applies to the old roses. To help you decide, the development of the car provides a useful analogy. Today, you can buy a new car: it is reliable and, if it goes wrong, the garage can fix it easily. Use it every day, pay it virtually no attention, it has all mod-cons and performs very well. Alternatively, you can buy an old car. There are a few that remain reliable and can be used every day. Many require additional attention and care, and you have to devote time, money and enthusiasm to them. They are a hobby, but not for every day use. They do not have all mod-cons, are slower, less refined and comfortable. If you want an easy-care garden with modern standards of performance, you should focus mainly on newer cultivars. If you have time and want a rewarding and absorbing hobby, then start a collection of both new and old roses. The properties that modern roses have in abundance over many of the older types are found in the areas summarized below.

Overall, newer cultivars will provide the easiest route to a colourful and easy-to-care for display. Just remember the improvements in features, performance and comfort of cars over the last century. Roses have improved in a similar way.

## Cultivars that suit your microclimate

Roses respond to local conditions in different ways. You should assess the following:

| | |
|---|---|
| Are the cultivars hardy in my area? | Pick only ones that are hardy enough |
| Do I live in an area of intense sunlight? | Avoid cultivars that fade or discolour in intense sunlight |
| Is my garden in an area that will suffer heavy rain during the flowering period? | Disregard cultivars with flowers that suffer in wet conditions |
| Will they be in a very windy position? | Don't go for cultivars that are too tall or have very large heavy flowers. |



| | |
|---|---|
| **Constitution** | The bush will have stronger stems and make more new stems from the base, giving a sturdy, strong plant. Modern cultivars will tend to be more vigorous than older ones. They combine vigour with plants that do not become too tall. |
| **Foliage** | Many modern cultivar have leaves that are placed more closely along the stem which makes the plant look more lush, with more leaf. |
| **Flower** | Modern cultivars produce a larger number of flowers in a flush, and very often they will repeat bloom more quickly. For the amount of colour provided they are streets ahead of most older cultivars. |
| **Health** | Many modern roses will be healthier than their older counterparts. Health is something that can never be guaranteed. It is subject to the physiological state of the plant. If the plant is under stress it will get disease. If it is growing without stress, its natural resistance will increase. Modern cultivars tend to have greater resistance than many of the older ones. |
| **Scent** | There are very few differences between modern and old. Both categories include a range – some are strongly scented, some have no scent, and most are in between. It is a myth that modern roses have no scent. Some roses have scent and some don't. That has always been true. |

*Above: Modern cultivars not only produce more flowers than older ones, but they have more dense and attractive foliage. The leaves are important – we look at them when the plant is not in flower.*

## Choosing the right size

As we have already noted (see page 16), size is fundamental if you want your roses to look right. A tall plant growing where a short one is needed (or vice versa) will always look wrong, and it will annoy you until you move it.

## The style

Formal, informal, modern, cottage, hybrid tea, floribunda, shrub there are numerous options. Don't be afraid to mix plants that others consider to come from divergent categories. The selection should reflect what you like, not what others ordain is acceptable. As in home decoration, one person's taste may be the antithesis of another's. Both are right, neither is wrong. What is right is for the individual to express their own taste in their own space.

## Colour

I always leave the selection of colour until last. I know that you will have decided early in the process that your ultimate desire is for, say, a ruby red rose but there is no point in looking at ruby red roses until you have established which type are suitable.

From the information you have already established, choose cultivars that will suit you

| | **Questions** | **Sample answers** |
|---|---|---|
| 1 | Modern or old? | Modern cultivar preferred |
| 2 | Suit my microclimate? | Can cope with strong sunlight |
| 3 | What size do I want? | Grows 1m (3ft) tall |
| 4 | The style? | Hybrid tea or floribunda |
| 5 | Colour? | Ruby red |

and will perform just as you want them to. You can add criteria that are important to you: health and scent are obvious candidates. The selection process may well lead to a degree of compromise, but we are dealing with nature and it is the case that nature cannot always provide us with exactly what we want. You may have to give way on colour in order to get the size you want, but that is a choice – making your own decisions on the priority of the various elements that create the whole.

It is much better to look for something when you know what you want. If you start looking for a red rose, you will find a vast array. Most of them will be unsuitable for one reason or another. The tighter your specification before you begin to look, the more successful you will be at achieving your goal.

# How to Buy

Roses are a part of our leisure and pleasures and there is no reason why buying them should not be a pleasure too. It is not like doing essential household shopping. This is a part of the wider experience of planning, design and enjoyment.

Rose cultivars are available a range of outlets. It is personal choice how you wish to buy, and my comments are only a guide.

## Rose specialist catalogues/ general nurseries

Many specialist growers produce catalogues. Some are illustrated, some rely on words. This is the route to the maximum choice. Do remember that they are catalogues and, as such, should be read as if they are the words of a salesman. The quality of service and plants will vary. Some are excellent, some barely acceptable.

## Garden centres

These are easy and convenient, and most people live close to a garden centre. They keep plants in stock for most of the year, catering for the 'instant' effect prevalent in so much modern retailing and advertising. Some garden centres provide a limited range of roses, and some a good range. The standard of rose care is usually lower than if you visit a nursery.



## Garden shows

Horticultural shows and exhibitions are great venues for getting ideas for seeing what is new and what is available in the market place, for finding new suppliers and for researching the plants. My personal advice would be not to order at a show unless you planned to do so before you left home. Everything is different at a show. The exhibits are staged and manicured and not at all natural. Exhibitors offer incentives to buy, and to their staff to sell. It can be a more pressurized purchase. You can lose track of scale: everything at an exhibition is big or oversized, which distorts your mind's view of the scale of your garden at home.

## Municipal or specialist gardens

Visiting gardens is an excellent way to investigate varieties. In most you will see how they grow and perform. In many you will also see how the variety looks not only at its best, but also at its worst. This is vital: roses all look good at their best, but some age gracefully, others disgracefully.

## Internet

The Internet will allow you to see a lot of roses. Most of the specialist nurseries have websites, many with on-line ordering. In addition to the specialists, there are general gardening sites that sell some roses. The pros and cons are similar to those for specialist nurseries and garden centres.

## Special offers

These are always very tempting, but you are buying what someone else wants to sell to you, not what you want. Take advantage or an offer if it suits you. If if it is not what you want, leave it alone.

## Nostalgia

Nostalgia can provide us with enjoyment or disappointment. Often, our memories are not as accurate as we would like to believe, and frequently we visualize the perfection of our grandparents' garden, with a beautiful rose that was always in flower, with a wonderful perfume. How we would love to try to recreate that ideal. Alas, it is rarely as we remember. The passage of time has corrupted our memories: the rose was not really in flower all the time, and the scent we recollect is the one we would like it to have been. We remember the ideal, not the reality, and even if we manage to track down the cultivar, it is likely to disappoint in our own garden.

## Friends' recommendations

Recent experience is better than vague memories. If you share the same objectives as a friend then this can work. If your friend spends more time on their roses than you are going to, then your results may not be so good. If your friend is competitive and you are not, do not get drawn in to comparisons. Try to create your own identity and just use what you see to be the best of your friend's choices or ideas.

## What to expect

There is one important aspect to remember: our roses are a hobby, we are growing them for pleasure. Part of that enjoyment should be the purchase of the plants. If you enjoy shopping for your plants and take time to find the cultivars you want and good-quality plants, it will be a big step towards overall satisfaction.

You should also understand what to expect when you buy roses. Shopping at garden centres is pretty straightforward: you look at the available plants, select the ones you want and take them home. Ordering from the Internet or a rose-grower's mail-order catalogue is different. As the consumer, you need to be sure that you understand all the details. The important issue is: when will the plants be delivered? Traditionally this is during the dormant period (autumn/winter/spring), when roses are despatched as bare-root plants. This means the plants are dug from the field and sent to you without any soil around them. So if you order in summer, your roses won't be delivered until autumn, and the plants will flower the following summer. However, if you order in winter, delivery will be almost immediate. The alternative, which is becoming more usual, that is for Internet and specialist growers to despatch pot-grown plants in season. This allows you to order in summer and receive the plants within a few days, making the service almost as quick as going to the local garden centre.

When your plants arrive is vital. Before you purchase or receive delivery there are a few basic tasks you should have completed. Have you decided where the plants will go? Have you checked that the natural conditions are suitable? Have you dug and fed the area to be planted? Have you removed any weeds that were growing there? Only when you can answer 'yes' to these questions are you ready for the plants. The last thing you want to do is to have them hanging around while you do the preparation. If they arrive before you are ready to plant you will rush the preparation and take short cuts, which will have a detrimental effect on your roses. 'Be prepared' – it makes it all a pleasure instead of a rush.



*Below: It is important to buy good plants. The plant on the left has had too many roots cut off while the one on the right looks as if it was stuffed (instead of potted) into a pot that is too small. It should not be sticking out of the pot like this.*

# The Growing Cycle

In this section we will look at the life of a rose, and identify the jobs you should do and the jobs you must do. We will start with planting, which is the beginning of the life cycle.

## Bare-root roses

Planting bare-root roses is the traditional way, and in many ways is still the best way. If you are to get the best from your new rose, make sure you carry out a few simple tasks.

## Check the quality before planting

Plants need a good root system and an adequate quantity of stems. They need to be free from material damage and obvious signs of disease. Start with the root system. It's not good if there is just one taproot. It's best if the root divides and branches out. We need plenty of fine roots, not a little coarse root. Two strong stems is all right, but not brilliant; three or more is best.

## Take care before planting



It is important to look after the plants between the time you get them and the time you plant them. Bare-root plants are very resilient, and they can withstand storage, transport and all manner of treatment that you would imagine to be damaging. Just think of where they would be in the natural world. Bare-root plants come in winter when they are dormant. Under natural conditions they would be outside, where it would be cold and frosty, wet and moist. That tells us how to keep them until we plant them. Keep them cold, out of direct sunlight and moist. They can be wrapped in wet newspaper and sealed in polythene bags and left somewhere cold (within about 5° of freezing) for at least three weeks. As soon as they begin to dry out they will begin to die. The two elements that cause drying are heat and air circulation. Although it is best to plant as soon as you can, if you have to store plants these are the conditions to do it in. Check that they are still moist and reseal the bag.

*Below: When buying bare-root roses, select those that have not had their roots chopped too short.*

## Planting time

Bare-foot roses can be planted at any time in autumn, winter and spring when the ground is not frozen hard. If an overnight frost clears by midday, carry on and plant.

## Planting method

Roses are easy to plant. All you need is reasonable conditions. I hope you will have prepared the site by digging it over, removing weeds and adding some well-rotted manure or compost. With the planting position prepared, all you have to do is dig a hole. It must be big enough to accommodate the roots of the plant. It can be a round or square, but make it deep enough – 25–30cm (10–12in) is sufficient. Put the plant into the hole. If you have to bend the roots a bit, that is fine, and trimming about 2.5cm (1in) off the ends can be helpful.

When the plant is sitting in the hole add a generous amount of compost soil. This will supply food and a good texture for the first new roots to penetrate. Wobble and shake the plant so that the compost falls between the roots. Replace half the soil, which should be friable and crumbly. Hold the stem of the plant with one hand to keep it at the right depth and then use your feet to tread the soil down to firm in the plant. Add the rest of the soil and tread in again, using all your weight.

1 *Dig a hole large enough. Don't worry if you bend the roots a little when you put the rose in the hole.*

2 *Put some good compost around the roots to give the roots a good stand in getting established.*

3 *When the hole is half-to-three quarters full of soil, carefully firm the soil with your foot.*

4 *Fill the hole and tread in again, making sure the planting is at the correct depth, then water well.*

*Above: A containerized or pot-grown climbing plant in early spring showing healthy new growth starting to appear.*

*Above: The root system holds the compost together and young white roots can be seen. It is not pot bound.*



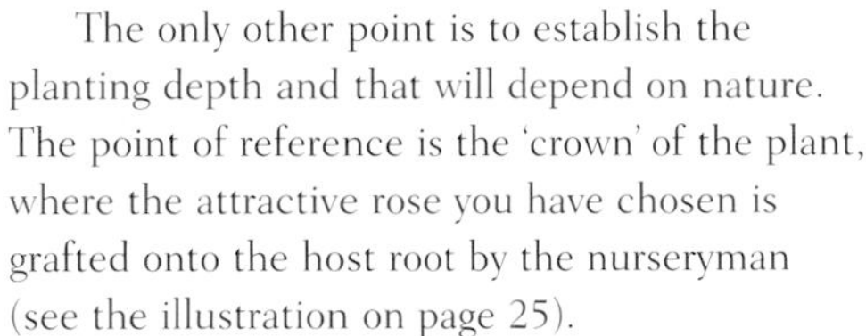

The only other point is to establish the planting depth and that will depend on nature. The point of reference is the 'crown' of the plant, where the attractive rose you have chosen is grafted onto the host root by the nurseryman (see the illustration on page 25).

The first variable provided by nature is your soil type. Is it a soil that drains quickly – a dry soil – or is it a soil that retains moisture and is wet? These are the two extremes. In dry conditions you can to plant the crown up to 5cm (2in) below the soil level. In wet soils keep the crown just above soil level. In average soil plant with the crown at ground level. If you plant too deeply in wet soils, the constant wet conditions will begin to rot the buried stems.

The second aspect of nature that will change the way you plant is if you are in an area with notoriously cold winters. Then you will need to protect the crown of the plant over winter. This can be with a mound of straw, soil or other insulating material. When the rose is happily planted there is one more task, water it in. Give at least 4.55 litres (1 gallon) of water for each plant. If conditions are dry and windy keep on watering into spring.

## Care after planting

If the planting is carried out in good soil, little immediate after care is required. Keep moist is the mantra that you must follow (see also pruning, page 34).

## Potential problems

There are no real problems associated with planting bare-root roses, only disbelief that a plant in such a naked, unprotected state will grow and thrive. Because the plant has no soil and no protection, there is an assumption that it will be weak and vulnerable. This is wrong, as long as the plants are kept in the right conditions before planting. Both you and the nursery that supplies the plant must keep the plants in good condition. If you are buying by mail order choose a good nursery that excels in plant quality, packaging and delivery. When bare-root roses are planted firmly and kept moist – which, with winter planting, is usually not too arduous –

then this is the easiest and best way of planting with a success rate of well over 90 per cent.

## Potted, pot-grown or containerized roses

CHECK THE QUALITY BEFORE PLANTING

Perhaps it is necessary to explain what a potted, pot-grown or containerized rose is. It is simply a bare-root rose that a nurseryman has dug out of the field and placed in a pot. It is as simple as that. The only reason for doing this is to satisfy consumer demand and to extend the planting season beyond the colder winter and spring months.

To check that you are buying good plants look at the plant and its foliage, the pot it is in and the compost. Do the plants look happy and have clean, green leaves? Are they bushy with strong stems? Are they new stock or left over from last year?

If you see any of the following don't buy the plant. Avoid plants with diseases such as downy mildew, powdery mildew, blackspot and rust (information on identifying these comes on pp 28-9). If a garden centre is selling plants with these ailments, go elsewhere. Insect pests such as caterpillars and greenfly are the most likely problems. If there are only a few on a plant, that is probably all right. If there are a lot, go elsewhere to purchase or point out the problem and tell the garden centre you will return in a few days, by which time the problem should have been sorted out.

Yellowing upper leaves can be a sign that the plant is undernourished. Healthy roses do not have a yellow tinge to the foliage.

There are three possible reasons for a rose to have yellowing lower leaves. The plants may be over watered or they may be packed so closely together that insufficient light penetrates to the foliage at the base. Roses can recover from either of these problems. The third reason is if the plant has blackspot or downy mildew – both of these form spots on the leaf, which will lose all its green colour and turn yellow. If the leaves are yellow with dark spots, don't buy the plant.

Moss or algae growing on the oldest stems at the base of the plant could indicate old stock. The plant could be pot bound, where the roots become too confined to the pot and go round in tight circles.

Next look at the pot. Is it big enough to support the plant? It should be a reservoir of food and water and not so small that it cramps the roots too much.

Look at the size. A 2-litre (6in) pot is too small and likely to be a waste of money, as most of the root will have to be cut off to get the plant into the pot.

The next size is 50 per cent bigger. A 3-litre (7in) pot is still on the small side, but adequate to sustain a plant into early summer. But when the plant begins to flower and demand higher levels of food and water, this size pot will inhibit its development.

The next is an increase of 33 per cent on the previous size – a 4-litre (8in) pot. This is the smallest pot that will sustain a plant in good condition. If the garden centre has a correct regime of maintenance then a plant in a pot this size is acceptable.

Larger pots offer more scope and potential for the plant to grow and develop without stress, and pots for roses can go up to 12 litres in size.

Finally, check the compost. It is the foundation of the plant, so it has to be good quality. If it dries out too quickly it will cause you difficulties in your garden. Does it contain a slow-release fertilizer to carry on feeding the plant? Is it free of weeds? Do not be afraid to ask the sales assistant to take a plant out of its pot. You will soon see whether it is well watered and if there is good root development.

As with bare-root roses, it is advisable to do the planting preparation before you buy the plants. However, if you have to keep the plants for a while before planting you must look after them. They will have come from a garden centre where plants are watered on a regular basis – at least once a day for most of the spring and summer periods. If you suddenly change its routine the plant will be upset. Keep plants well watered every day.

PLANTING TIME

In theory, potted plants can be planted at any time of year as long as the soil is not frozen hard. Very hot and dry weather can also stress the plants.

#### PLANTING METHOD

Assuming the soil is prepared and in good condition, planting is easy. Start by giving the pot a good soaking. Dig a hole that is a little larger than the pot. Make sure the soil at the base of the hole is friable or crumbly and then add a little planting compost. Remove the plant from the pot and place it carefully in the hole and replace earth around it, using a mixture of soil and compost. Tread in firmly on all sides and water well. The planting depth is the same for both pot-grown and bare-root roses: adjust it according to the type of soil in your garden.

#### CARE AFTER PLANTING

Pot-grown roses will require more care than bare-root roses if they are to become established quickly and successfully. Earlier in this book I compared the soil's relationship to a rose with the foundations of a building. When we take a plant from a pot we are bound to disturb the soil around the delicate root structure, and placing it into different soil can be nothing short of a cultural shock – like picking up a building from a city and placing it in the wilderness. To counter this shock is very simple: water. If the ambient conditions are dry, water on a regular basis for the first four weeks – and remember the plant was accustomed to daily watering in the garden centre and will expect similar tretment in its new environment. In the medium term, check that there is no shrinkage of the compost that the plant was grown in. Sometimes the compost that the plant was grown in will dry out and shrink, but the soil in the garden will not shrink. When this happens a gap develops between the original rootball of the plant and the garden soil. Water will not travel between the two properly and the plant will dry out and die, so fill any gap with soil and water.

#### POTENTIAL PROBLEMS

If the right amount of water is administered, planting potted roses will be successful. You should achieve close to 100 per cent success. If the plants are poor or have suffered before planting the success rates will plummet to about 66 per cent.

## On-going rose care

I will leave pruning until the next section of the book and start with early and mid-season care. This is the period that starts after pruning and finishes as the first flowers begin to open.

There is good news here for there is little to do. If you have done the preparation and planting carefully, the plants will be largely self-managing. However, we still have to pay attention to them and respond to the conditions that nature provides.

#### MOISTURE

If there is a dry spell, then water. I always advise watering early in the day if possible. Evening watering encourages greater night-time humidity, which can lead to disease.

#### FROST

Where late frosts damage the lush new shoots of spring, treat them as described on page 14.

#### WIND

If the wind is violent it can cause damage by making branches rub together or by snapping young shoots. Cut out damaged shoots to protect against disease.

We can add things to improve results. A mulch of bark, well-rotted manure or other organic material will keep the plant roots cool and moist. It can also be effective at keeping weeds down, which keeps up appearances and reduces work. Roses like lots of food. Add a fertilizer to boost growth prior to flowering.

Be vigilant and spot early signs of trouble. There is a range of fungi whose spores travel on the wind and spread diseases liable to attack roses. They are listed and described here in their likely order of appearance during the season.

## Diseases affecting foliage

#### DOWNY MILDEW

This is often a problem where air circulation is poor. It likes humidity, warm days and cold nights and it tends to attack young foliage, creating irregular marks on the leaves. The marks very dark, but when held up to the light have a slight purple hue. As the fungus grows the leaf turns yellow before it falls from the plant. Downy mildew is most common before the flowers open. Avoid the problem by choosing resistent cultivars and by growing the plants well so that they are stress free and have maximum natural resistance. Good ventilation around the leaves and keeping the soil moist help, as finally does the application of an effective fungicide.

### RUST

Most modern roses have a strong resistance to rust. It is another fungus whose spores travel by air. The first sign will be pustules, two or three times the size of a pinhead, on the underside of the leaves. These give the fungus its name as they are rust coloured, turning black with time. It tends to attack leaves on the lower part of the plant, but its presence will be noticeable from the upper leaves as the veins turn yellow. The leaves will fall off after a severe attack. This is another fungus that enjoys wetter conditions. Damage is caused not only to the leaves, but to the stem where the leaf joins it. It can prevent the auxiliary bud from that leaf node developing into a strong shoot in the future. There are proprietary products for preventing the spread of rust.

### POWDERY MILDEW

Although this is often the most noticeable of the fungal diseases, in many ways it is the least damaging. It is unsightly, yes, but not threatening to the life of the plant. It is the common white powdery substance that appears very often on young growth in the second half of the season. It is more prevalent in hot dry summers. Either put up with it or use a treatment from a garden centre.

*Below: A rose with powdery mildew, which looks like white powder on the leaves.*

BLACKSPOT

This is a problem on older leaves but will not normally be seen until after the first flush of flowers is over. Keep an eye on the lower leaves. As its name suggests, it will appear as black spots on the leaves. In appearance it is similar to downy mildew, except it tends to form on older foliage first. The spots are black and close to a perfect circle in shape. In time the leaves will turn yellow and fall prematurely.

## Controlling disease

There is a common thread running through the management of these diseases – think about nature. The first and best defence against disease is to have a plant that is growing with vigour. The plant is just like you and me: under stress we are more susceptible to illness and so are plants. Many natural occurrences can trigger stress, including poor soil, drought, uneven watering, waterlogging, poor light, poor feeding and, finally, exhaustion. You may consider this last factor a strange concept for plants, but it happens when a plant has produced a mass of flowers. Flowering uses a lot of energy, food and water. Remember that the objective of all plants and animals is to breed. The flower is no more than an exotic display to attract the bees that do the pollination to further the species. We all know the effort teenagers put into looking just right and how tired they are after a week of discos and parties. Roses are the same after flowering, so give them a boost. Feed them just before they come into flower (remember it takes time for the fertilizer to get down to the roots), so that they benefit and recover quickly from the effort of flowering.

Disease management can be accomplished by providing good soil, site, planting and after care, but you must also observe the plants. If one plant is susceptible to disease every year, it will always be the first to suffer and spread the disease. There is a good argument for removing that particular plant. This is little more than natural selection: in nature the weakest of the species will perish. Why not copy nature in the garden? To me it is a successful, if sometimes ruthless, model to follow.

At this stage we reach one of the points at which different gardeners will proceed in different ways. The choices are to accept a small level of disease and do nothing; to attempt to reduce any disease with organic methods; or to try to control disease with fungicides.

I have to say that in principle it is bad gardening practice to grow diseased plants in the garden, because there can be a build-up over a number of years, making control harder and harder. On the other hand in a leisure/pleasure garden I do not believe that it is essential to control disease completely. In the most natural sense there is a place on earth for both the plant and the disease that is a parasite on it.

In gardening terms, the analogy I use to imagine a plant under stress should work both

*Left: The fungus that causes blackspot makes round, black marks on the leaves, which will then turn yellow and fall off.*

ways. Is it worth the human stress of trying to keep the plants in a perfect condition? To do so requires a dedication that goes beyond leisure and can become pressure. When a hobby becomes a source of worry it will cease to be so much of a pleasure. It is natural for a parasite and its host to cohabit, so my view is that a low level of managed disease is acceptable in the leisure garden.

There are numerous organic potions that can help to keep plants healthy. The chemical fungicide market is in constant turmoil with many deletions from the range. Use chemicals to control severe outbreaks and to stop the spread of the disease. Make sure you always use a proprietary treatment that is appropriate to the disease you are trying to control, and follow the manufacturer's instructions about quantities, frequency of application and timing.

## Insect damage

The next area of control is to limit the damage caused by insects. This too has to be taken to the level that you are content with. To keep all insects away all of the time is virtually impossible, and it is usually better to accept that there are insects about and just try to limit any overly serious attacks. The worst insects are described here.

### APHIDS

Greenfly commonly visit roses, black and white fly less often. The damage from these insects occurs as they suck sugar solution from the plant. They keep sucking the plant's sugars out even when they have had enough, so it passes through them and becomes a sticky mess on the leaves and around the flower buds.

This causes two problems. The aphids are eating the food that the plant has made for itself, while the sticky sugary deposits are an easy surface for a fungus, sooty mould, to stick to and gain an initial foothold to infest the plant. Greenfly multiply very quickly. Having an unusual lifestyle, in which the male is not required for reproduction, they breed at an astounding rate. A large colony will make a mess of a plant, making it unattractive and sticky to touch.

There are many forms of control, all of which will work to some degree. It is worth experimenting with planting companion plants such as African marigolds, which can deter aphids. Although aphids blow around on the wind, they have enough flight control to decide whether to visit your garden or one further down the road. Prevention has to be worth a try.

The second method is to encourage natural controls. Other insects and some birds feed on aphids. Ladybirds and hoverflies are particularly keen on them, so encourage more beneficial insects into your garden by growing plants, such as solidago and many of the daisy-like species, that provide these insects with easy access to nectar. Then there is spraying. A weak solution of washing-up liquid can help by breaking down

*Right: Aphids – commonly called greenfly – suck the sugary sap from the plant, making the flower bud and stem sticky.*

the surface tension of the water, which will then form a film rather than individual droplets, and this film of water will suffocate the aphids. A jet of water from a hose will wash off a small group of greenfly. The alternative is to use a commercial insecticide.

RED SPIDER MITE

This is a destructive little insect. The individual mites are tiny, best seen through a magnifying glass. They lay thousands of eggs on the underside of the leaves and the eggs are more visible than the adults. The leaf takes on a bronzed, sickly hue. Red spider mites will appear in warm, dry spots. They love plants that are growing against a wall and plants that are densely covered with small leaves, but they will also attack plants with big leaves. They make the plant look sick, starting with leaves low down and working their way upwards. Red spider mites hate water, and high-pressure squirts of water on the underside of the leaf will slow progress.



WESTERN FLOWER THRIP

As the name suggests, these thrips are interested in flowers. They prefer warmer climates but are becoming more common in Britain. Thrips are tiny – the next size up from the thunder fly and much smaller than a greenfly. They get into the flower buds and eat the petals. As the flowers open, all the petals will have a disfigured brown edge, be shortened and generally look a mess. Use a chemical control.

POLLEN BEETLE

These are harmless to the plant but unpleasant to us. The small black beetles are an agricultural pest, which live on the yellow flowers of oil seed rape. However, that crop stops flowering just before roses bloom, when the pollen beetle looks for another home. Roses are one of the subjects they choose, especially the yellows, whites and some orange shades. Look before you sniff, unless you enjoy beetles up your nose.

CATERPILLARS

The young of moths and butterflies will munch away at rose leaves and, if there are a lot of them, they can leave the foliage in tatters. I never like destroying all caterpillars, because some grow into magnificent and beautiful adult butterflies. Nature offers a partial cure as birds will eat some; chemical control will stop them ruining your plants completely.

SAWFLY

The leaf-rolling sawfly is adept at winding up rose growers. The adults live in trees – part of a copse or woodland – and rarely in gardens. Adult flies visit rose bushes to lay eggs on the leaves. The female poisons each leaf that she lays an egg on, causing it to roll up as neatly as a cigar. By making a tightly rolled tube, the sawfly creates a safe and protected home for its egg, out of sight of predators and protected from the weather. Many leaves on a plant can be infected. Apart from the strange appearance – it does little harm. The leaf will still feed the rose. It is hard to treat, as the instigator of the complaint is just a visitor for a moment to lay her eggs. Either pick the leaves off or ignore them completely.

## Managing insect pests

With the exception of greenfly, which breed without the assistance of a partner, it is often essential to deal with insects twice. A little understanding of an insect's lifecycle helps. Adults lay eggs, which go through an adolescent (too-young-to-breed) stage before they mature. If on a given day there are some insects at each stage and you use a treatment, it will be effective on the adults and adolescents. Even if you had 100 per cent success, another generation will hatch from the eggs and develop through the adolescent stage to adults in a few days. The second treatment needs to catch those adolescents before they mature and lay another generation of eggs. If you do a little research and find out what you are battling against, the battle will be far easier to win.

## Other pests

Hundreds of different insects may visit your roses. Many of them are harmless, appear only for a few days or do limited damage. Small populations of insects will not do anything like as much harm as small mammals, such as deer, rabbits or hares, which can strip the leaves and bark from the plant. The best long-term protection from this type of wildlife is fencing. Deer are particularly partial to new young shoots in spring but winter damage can be far worse. When there is only a limited amount of food available, hares and rabbits can strip the bark from the stems of the roses at ground level. This can be treated only by cutting out the damaged wood. When the bark is stripped, there is an open wound into the heart of the plant. The wound will become infected and a weak point unless it is removed.

## Tasks for the growing season

There are two other growing season tasks. Repeat flowering uses lots of energy, so remember to feed plants to keep them healthy. The second task is deadheading, which also helps to conserve a plant's energy. When a flower has finished blooming the ovary remains and it will turn into a seed pod. The sole objective of a plant is to propagate itself, by forming seeds in a seed pod. Deadheading achieves two results. Stopping the plant from forming a seed pod means the plant thinks; 'Hey, no seed, no offspring. I will have to make more flowers to produce another crop of seed.' And that is just what we wanted – more flowers. Deadheading is also linked to seed production. Producing a seed pod is a bit like a pregnancy – it takes a lot of energy from the mother. If we prevent seed pods from forming, the plant will put more effort into producing better growth, and more growth means more flowers.

Our final annual task is pruning. Most of the work in the growing season is common sense. Plan the position, give the plants enough space and air, good soil, make a good choice of cultivars and plant them well. If you get these prerequisites right, future work is immeasurably reduced. Regular feeding and watering will be your main tasks to assure great results.

*Below: Once this caterpillar has fully matured it will eat most of these leaves.*

# Pruning

There is only one statement that I want to make at the start of this section, because I know people think pruning is complicated, difficult and confusing: in my view it is far better to give it a go and achieve a partial success than not try at all.

Pruning is actually quite easy. Let's start with explaining why we do it. I would like to borrow from nature to help me. Before mankind cultivated roses – indeed, before mankind – roses were pruned, not in an accurate or precise fashion, but by the environment they lived in. As a result of the harsh treatment dished out by nature, roses thrived and spread across the globe. There is a hint in here: harsh treatment works. In nature pruning could take place in a number of ways. Frost may have killed off many canes on a plant, grazing animals could cut them down, lightening might start a fire or a large tree felled by the wind could indiscriminately crush the branches of a rose below. There are many more ways in which plants could be cut back by nature, but the idea I want to express is that it is the act of cutting back that is important – the precision of the cut is secondary.



What is the point of pruning? It benefits both the plant and the gardener.

For the plant it is all about vigour, vitality and virility. When a plant is young it produces stems full of energy. As a stem ages it becomes similar to an aged and damaged artery. The wall is clogged with years of deposits; it is not as flexible as it was, and it is no longer an efficient working part. An old stem cannot supply enough fluids from the roots to the top of the plant. This will limit the number of flowers and the pleasure the plant gives us, as well as the ease with which it can reproduce. As the plant wants to reproduce, it encourages any means to prevent this ageing process – how very human. In the wild that method is pruning by uncontrolled external influences. By removing sections of the old stems the plant reduces the distance over which it has to carry fluids through old and internally damaged stems. It allows it to generate more young and virile stems from ground level.

To understand pruning it helps if we know how a plant grows. All the way along a stem there are little 'nodes' from which the leaves grow. At each of these nodes is an auxiliary bud. This type of bud grows into a new shoot. If a shoot has 20 sets of leaves along its length, then it has 20 auxiliary buds as well. Left unpruned, the plant will grow from the uppermost of these buds: in our example it will shoot from the twentieth bud first, that is, the highest one. This bud is on the thinnest, uppermost part of the stem. The plant has to transport food for the bud to the very end of the stem. The shoot that grows from this point will be tall, subject to wind damage and weak – it cannot be any fatter or stronger than the tip of the stem it is growing from.

1 *A mature bush rose that has been regularly pruned in the past.*

If we know where the plant will grow from, we can understand that if we cut a length of the stem away, and leave four or five of these auxiliary buds on the stem, we solve all the potential problems of leaving a rose unpruned.

Now we can start pruning and get expert results. Please bear in mind that these comments on pruning are generalizations, and there will be circumstances where you will have to do something different to gain a specific result. First, we need to set out our objectives to enable us to visualize the end result which is to have a plant

**2** *After the removal of the dead, diseased, weak and damaged wood, all that is left are good stems.*

**3** *The finished result after the good stems are pruned back.*



that is strong and healthy. Pruning will promote stronger, vigorous growth, able to resist disease.

We want to create growth that will support plenty of flowers. Young, youthful and vigorous growth means an increased ability to flower.

Pruning also stops the plant from getting leggy. When a plant is said to be leggy it means that there is a lot of old, woody growth at the base of the plant that lacks leaf cover. It looks as if the productive bit of the plant is stuck up on stilts or legs. Pruning prevents this from happening and stops the plant getting taller and taller every year.

Finally pruning increases the productive life of the plant. By promoting more young growth from low down, the amount of heavily aged wood is reduced, increasing the lifespan of the plant.

## When to prune

Timing depends on climate. In warm areas pruning starts early, in cold climates it is later. Don't be tempted to start too early. After pruning plants make new young shoots that are the future of the plant, and you do not want to risk losing them to a late frost. It is better to prune late than too early. The penalty for late pruning is minimal, and the difference between pruning at the start and pruning at the end of spring will be indiscernible in plant quality. All that happens is the early pruning will get the roses to bloom about four or five days earlier. That is all the difference it makes. Early pruning carries more risk of damage to the new shoots from a late frost. Be patient (which is one of nature's virtues) and wait until it is safe to prune. In all areas there is a pruning window of around six weeks in spring. If your garden is in a frost pocket, wait and prune later. If your roses suffer from downy mildew.in early spring, try pruning a bit later – it will mean that there is less foliage at the time of an early attack, and as a result the plant may be more resistant. Finally, experiment: stagger your pruning and see what suits your garden best.

## Best practice

No matter when you prune your rose plants, there are some guidlines to observe that will give some good results.

1 *This damaged wood needs to be cut out in the annual prune.*

2 *Cut below the damage no matter how low you have to go*

3 *The aim is to have a well-balanced rose with an open centre and good shape.*

4 *When you cut through the stem the inside should be white. If there is brown discolouration cut it out.*

- Always use good sharp secateurs. A sharp blade gives a clean cut and takes less effort.
- Try to make the cut about 1.25cm (0.5in) above an auxiliary bud.
- Make a sloping cut so that water will not sit on top of it or drain onto the auxiliary bud.
- Always cut out damaged stems.
- Try to prune into last summer's growth.
- Cut out any weak stems, making allowances for the fact that some cultivars have more slender stems than others. Some have a heavy build, some a lighter framework.

## Pruning specific types of plants

Let's start with newly planted roses. If you have planted bare-root roses over winter or in spring, prune as follows.

- Bush roses (hybrid tea and floribunda): cut all the stems down to about the length of your index finger.
- Patio and border roses: prune to leave all the stems no longer than your forefinger.
- Climbing and shrub roses: prune the stems so that they are between 15–23cm (6–9in ) tall.

For new plants, that's it.

## Pruning established plants

All the general observations we have made up to now apply to established roses, but there is the additional requirement of visualizing how we want the plant to look. In our Utopian vision the plant is freely branching, well clothed with foliage, a neat and even shape, with branches growing densely but without intermingling and damaging each other. Our task is to turn the vision into a reality.

### BUSH ROSES (HYBRID TEA AND FLORIBUNDA ROSES)

Gone are the old days when these roses needed to be treated in different ways. Modern floribunda roses can be treated in the same way as to hybrid teas. It will make virtually no difference whether it is a plant that will grow up to 1m (3ft) or 1.8m (6ft) tall.

Start by looking at the plant and picturing in your mind's eye the way you want it to look in the summer. How does it look now? Is it

1 *These established roses are ready for pruning.*

2 *The first stage is to remove the dead, damaged, diseased and weak growth.*

3 *The pruned roses. Make sure that you end up with a balanced shape.*

lopsided, is it getting leggy or is it bushy? Is the centre overcrowded? Is there any dead, diseased or damaged wood to cut out?

Having imagined the shape we want to achieve, now is the time to start cutting. First, take out dead wood because it is obviously useless – and the thorns on dead wood often hurt more than live thorns. Next remove any weak growth. Then remove anything that is clearly damaged. This includes cutting out any wood where the pith in the centre of the stem is brown. Brown pith means a damaged stem. Keep cutting down until you get to white pith, even if you have to go all the way to the base of the plant. Remove any old growth that looks past its 'sell-by date.'

All that is left now is growth that has good potential. Check your mental picture of the shape of the plant and revise it if necessary at this stage.

We now change tack and select the best growths. These are the lovely strong branches that are young and full of vitality. Now comes the first tricky bit: identifying last year's growth, which is easy with practice. These stems had flowers on last summer; they should start fairly low on the plant and will usually still be young looking, not brown and gnarled. When you find them, cut back hard, leaving them 10–20cm (4–8in)long. Try to cut at an angle above an auxiliary bud. These buds are spaced regularly up the stem and are arranged in an alternate pattern. If you can see two buds, there will also be one on the other side of the branch, in between the two you can see.

Bear in mind that the top bud you leave is likely to grow a new shoot – the plant invariably shoots from the highest auxiliary bud on the stem. Make sure you cut to one that is pointing in roughly the direction you want it to grow in.

If you are trying to rescue old roses you must behave differently. If roses have not had any pruning or if the pruning was too light for many years, plants will have old wood, bare lower stems and unattractive, weak spindly, top growth. You may have to cut into the old hard gnarled wood

*Left: A shrub rose will have many flower clusters at the same time. The effect is stunning when there are so many flowers together.*

*Above: Roses are perfect for combining with other plants – in this garden we can see climbing, shrub and hybrid tea roses.*



and hope that it will shoot (it doesn't always). If you do try this, prune into the old wood at least two months earlier than you would normally, regardless of any frosts.

### PATIO AND BORDER BUSH ROSES

These are more compact in their growing habit than other bush roses. The general mistake made in pruning is to think that because they are small plants they are delicate little specimens and require only the lightest of pruning. Dispel that thought: they are hardy and tough and love to be chopped down hard each year.

Because the growing habit is to produce a myriad of densely packed stems from the base and for those stems to branch very freely, giving the rounded, floriferous habit that we like, we do have to change the rules a little. With the multi-branching varieties it is not worth looking to see which direction a bud is pointing. There are so many, so close together that the law of averages wins out. Cut back hard and it will be fine. We can be less strict about crossing branches. After all they are compact, short plants, so the wind will not blow them about and rub the stems together.

The method should be to cut out all the weak, damaged and dead wood. Cut down all the strong stems from last year's growth to 8–13cm (3–5in). Trim the remainder to be neat, tidy but not too overcrowded. Job done.

### SHRUB ROSES

Pruning shrub roses offers plenty of scope for individual freedom and choice. Some of the modern shrub roses can be pruned in the same way as bush roses (hybrid tea and floribunda), except you should be less severe – say, cut off between one-half and two-thirds of last season's growth.

The alternative method for most of the older shrub roses is different. You need to start in the same way by removing dead, diseased and very weak growth. The next step is to trim lightly – more like a hair cut than a massacre. Trim to make the plant the size and shape that you want it to be. This allows the plant to adopt a dense, informal but soft shape which is frequently suited to these older cultivars. Every four or five years you should prune harder to encourage young growth to regenerate from the base of the plant.

### CLIMBING AND RAMBLING ROSES

It is common practice to prune climbers and ramblers in early autumn. This allows you to train in new growth and prune at the same time – doing two jobs at once seems like a good idea.

The important task with a climber is to get the structure covered. It is best to train branches in any direction except vertically (unless you want them to go straight up). On a wall take good strong branches and create a fan. On a pillar or post, train the stem to go round and round the post to form a spiral. There is a reason for not allowing the rose to grow vertically. Earlier we looked at the way it is always the last auxiliary bud on the stem that grows. If your climber has a stem that goes up to 1.8–3m (6–10ft), only the last bud on that stem will grow a shoot. The way we get the plant to grow from lots of the buds along the stem is by training the stem towards the horizontal and away from the vertical. In this way most of the auxiliary buds will shoot out short flowering stems. By fanning, spiralling, bending and weaving we get the effect that we want – a framework covered in short flowering growths.

Now trim back the short flowering laterals to within 2.5cm (1in) of the main stem. Train any new climbing shoots into a suitable gap in the framework. If possible, use a new shoot to replace one of the old ones. If the stems are too long, shorten them to make them fit the space you have. Try not to prune climbers too hard which can cause lots of growth and few flowers.

*Below: A mature shrub rose. This specimen of 'Nevada' is at least 2.7m (9ft) tall and 3.6m (12ft) wide.*

*Above, right: Climbers can be used on different structures.*
*Below, right: Many ramblers bear dense clusters of small flowers.*

# bush roses
# floribunda

# Amber Queen

## Bush Rose (Floribunda)

### FLOWER PROPERTIES ★★★★★

**Colour**

I cannot think of another rose with such a pure colour to its flower. Clean, bright and a delightful deep amber, only in the very hottest of sun will we begin to see the depth of the colour fade towards a golden-yellow. It always excels in sunny sites, and there can be some flower damage in wetter climates.

**Size and Shape**

The buds are conical in shape, opening into cupped blooms with around 30 petals. The blooms average 6.5cm (2.5in) in diameter.

**Scent**

Well perfumed: there are hints of apple and lemon in the fragrance.

**Production**

The clusters of flower are usually no more than five buds. The centre bloom is always the largest, but all are attractive. This is a cultivar that will begin to flower earlier in the season than average and will repeat well throughout.

### PLANT PROPERTIES ★★★★

**Shape and Size**

Short, compact and dense in its growing habit. It makes lots of basal growth and benefits from hard pruning. In very windy sites the weight of the flowers can be too much for the stems to hold upright. In most gardens expect a height of 75cm (2.5ft) and a width of 60cm (2ft).

**Position**

Will thrive in any open position. Partial sunlight is acceptable

**Hardiness**

Survives well in most regions. Avoid areas with low light levels.

### FOLIAGE PROPERTIES ★★★★

**Colour**

One of the additional beauties is the rich purple of the young foliage. It soon changes to green with bronze undertones.

**Health Check**

In very dry, hot summers there may be some powdery mildew. Overall, the health is good, and if you keep the plant happy it will reward you.

**Garden Uses**

Anywhere, from mixed borders to formal rose gardens.

### OVERALL ASSESSMENT ★★★★

- ✔ Colour and ease of management in the garden.
- ✖ Needs correct location – avoid anywhere windy. Flowers will be smaller if it is sunny.

# Baby Love

## Bush Rose (Floribunda)

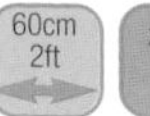

### FLOWER PROPERTIES ★★★

**Colour**

Bright yellow. This is one of those flowers that leaves me speechless. The colour is simple, bright yellow.

**Size and Shape**

The flowers are small, only 2.5cm (1in) across. They pop open very quickly from small round buds, and very soon you have a fully open, simple single, five-petalled flower.

**Scent**

There is no appreciable scent from the individual blooms.

**Production**

Generous in the production of flowers, maximizing the flowering season by starting to bloom early. The clusters have numerous buds. I find that there is little point in counting beyond 50 buds in a cluster, by then we know that there are a lot and that it will keep flowering well over a good period.

### PLANT PROPERTIES ★★★

**Shape and size**

Diminutive in stature, it develops into a small rounded shrublet, and the shape is one of its assets, as with a rounded shape we get bloom low down. Unlikely to be above 60cm (2ft) tall in most areas and may be as wide as it is tall.

**Position**

Will thrive in any open position where there is no exposure to cold winter winds.

**Hardiness**

Good in warm and hot regions. Not so hardy in the coldest areas.

### FOLIAGE PROPERTIES ★★★★★

**Colour**

The leaves are tiny and numerous, fully clothing the bush. The colour is reassuring to look at, dark green and glossy – a combination that always makes for an attractive bush and contrasts well with the bright yellow flowers.

**Health Check**

Acclaimed as a healthy variety, specifically bred to be healthy. So far it is showing good resistance to disease.

**Garden Uses**

Try it in a pot, border or bed.

### OVERALL ASSESSMENT ★★★★

✔ Good health. Compact neat habit.

✖ Flowers go over quickly.

# Betty Boop

## Bush Rose (Floribunda)

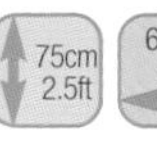

FLOWER PROPERTIES ★★★★★

**Colour**

This is a bicolour: the flower is split into zones of contrasting colour. The centre is cream, while the edge of the flower has a carmine rim. As the flower ages the cream fades to be closer to white and the carmine intensifies, spreading towards the base of the petal. A tough flower, which is resistant to weather damage. In hotter sites the amount of red will increase more quickly as the flower ages.

**Size and Shape**

Plump buds open to reveal a tall, long flower with the carmine rim and cream below. The blooms open wide, over 8cm (3in) in diameter, with 15 petals.

**Scent**

The perfume is light, somewhere between apple and aniseed.

**Production**

In this aspect there are no faults. The flowering season starts early and repeat blooms allow our enjoyment to continue to the very end of the season. The clusters have plenty of flowers, that are well spaced and open over several days.

PLANT PROPERTIES ★★★★

**Shape and Size**

A compact, neat plant. It will provide a bushy specimen of even growth. In average conditions expect a height of 75cm (2ft 6in) and 60cm (2ft) wide.

**Position**

Very strong sunlight will affect the colour, otherwise it will go anywhere in the garden.

**Hardiness**

Good in most regions. Give protection In severe winters.

FOLIAGE PROPERTIES ★★★

**Colour**

Starting with a plum leaf, which matures to dark green. A shine to the leaf leads us to expect good health.

**Health Check**

Overall, a reliable performer but will require good culture to keep healthy. Blackspot can attack if the plant is under stress.

**Garden Uses**

Anywhere – in pots, tubs, beds, borders – it is sure to be a pleasure.

OVERALL ASSESSMENT ★★★★

✔ The effect and quantity of the flowers will bring weeks of enjoyment.

✖ Weak perfume and imperfect health.

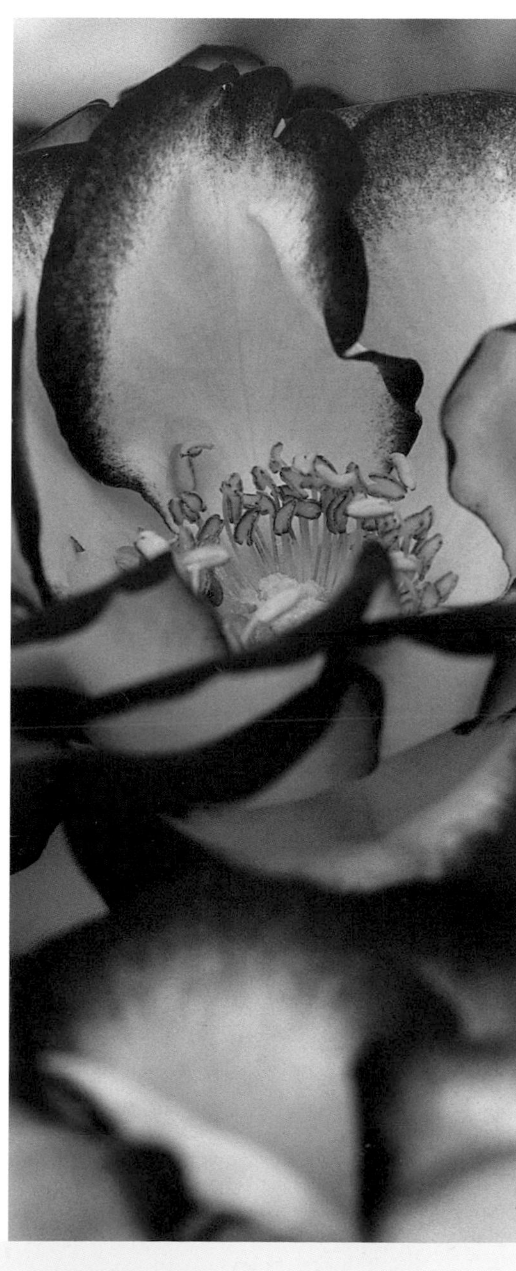

# Betty Harkness

## Bush Rose (Floribunda)

zone
6–7

### FLOWER PROPERTIES ★★★★★

**Colour**

Tough to put into words, but it is a tangerine with a little red added. It is powerful, attractive and striking. For such a strong shade it has a very stable colour, hardly fading at all as the flower ages.

**Size and Shape**

The plump, dark green buds open to reveal a flower of exquisite beauty. Initially the flower has a classic shape with the ever-desirable pointed bud, which opens slowly into a cupped flower. The size is good, at well over 8cm (3in ) across, with over 30 petals.

**Scent**

Strong and a delight. The classic sweet rose perfume.

**Production**

With clusters of up to nine buds, a prolific flower production throughout the season – the recipe for a wonderfully colourful cultivar.

### PLANT PROPERTIES

**Shape and Size** ★★★★★

This is a strong growing plant, without becoming difficult to manage. Producing plenty of basal shoots, it is easy to create a fine bush specimen. It will produce a bush that is about 1.1m (3ft 6in) tall and 75cm (2ft 6in) wide.

**Position**

No problem here: as long as it is in a light position it will be happy.

**Hardiness**

A tough plant, it is worth trying in any region. Tolerates extremes remarkably well.

### FOLIAGE PROPERTIES

**Colour** ★★★★

Leaves are a very dark green, robust-looking and thick, giving a rich, effulgent appearance.

**Health Check**

Not quite perfect but acceptable. Blackspot may appear when the plant is growing under stress.

**Garden Uses**

Anywhere a strong colour is wanted in traditional rose gardens; or use it as an individual plant.

### OVERALL ASSESSMENT ★★★★

✔ Perfume and general good behaviour. Good as a cut flower.

✖ The colour may be too strong for some schemes or tastes.

# Cream Abundance
## Bush Rose (Floribunda)

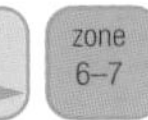


FLOWER PROPERTIES ★★★★★

**Colour**

A combination of off-whites and creams intensifies towards the centre of the flower. In very sunny conditions flowers fade before petal fall, but only to white, which is quite attractive. For a pale colour the petals are very resistant to rain damage – brown spots are rare.

**Size and Shape**

Before opening the buds become plump and rounded. Initially a little flat, as the flower opens the shape develops to a lovely circular one with over 50 petals. It retains a tight centre, thus extending the time of maximum beauty.

**Scent**

A pleasing perfume – a combination of myrrh and apple.

**Production**

A lot of flowers for the space taken. Clusters of seven to nine buds open over a period of weeks and are rapidly followed by subsequent flushes of flower.

PLANT PROPERTIES ★★★★

**Shape and Size**

Exudes vitality and a desire to grow. Growing to just below average height for a bush rose, it is bushy, compact and sturdy. Shoots from the base are strong and the flowering side shoots have plenty of rigidity to hold the flowers upwards. The plant produces a rounded form, 75cm (2ft 6in) high and 60cm (2ft) wide.

**Position**

It likes to thrive and will do so in most positions, even those that are challenging.

**Hardiness**

It will require some protection in the very coldest regions but anywhere else is fine. ★★★★★

FOLIAGE PROPERTIES

**Colour**

The leaves are quite large and are a rich, dark green. They look wonderful on the plant, even when there are no flowers. They are a delectable contrast to the flowers.

**Health Check**

Resistance to ailments is good. As late season approaches some blackspot may be seen.

**Garden Uses**

From mixed borders to formal rose gardens.

OVERALL ASSESSMENT ★★★★

✔ All the components go together to make a wonderful plant.

✖ Not a popular colour, but one that brings out the best in mixed colour schemes.

# Easy Going

## Bush Rose (Floribunda)

### FLOWER PROPERTIES ★★★★★

**Colour**

Somewhere in the region that falls between amber and gold, this is a colour that brings a smile to your face. It is rich and pure, restful yet bright. I am always astounded at the stability of the colour in all weather conditions. As the flower ages there is a faint infusion of rose pink.

**Size and Shape**

The buds are light green, opening to reveal what appears to be a yet smaller bud, with the outer petals showing the slight pink hue that returns as the flowers die. From these unpromising buds the petals unfurl and enlarge to provide a divine flower in colour and form. On maturity the flower will be up to 10cm (4in) in diameter, with 30 petals arranged in perfect symmetry.

**Scent**

The sweet and fruity perfume not the strongest but is still a pleasure.

**Production**

A cultivar that enjoys flowering. It starts early in the season and finishes late. The clusters are of five or seven blooms, and they just keep on coming. Well worth using as cut flowers – after all, the bush will just produce more.

### PLANT PROPERTIES ★★★★★

**Shape and Size**

A very neat and even bush. The flowers are held up on stems that have plenty of strength, growing to an even height and making a pretty rounded canopy. The plant will mature to be no more than 1m (3ft) tall and 60cm (2ft) wide.

**Position**

In all garden positions except shaded areas.

**Hardiness**

Thrives in all but the coldest regions, where it will survive if it is given winter protection.

### FOLIAGE PROPERTIES ★★★★

**Colour**

Light green foliage with a deep shine. The leaves are a good size and provide an attractive foil to the flower colour. Lots of leaves are produced, making it an attractive foliage plant.

**Health Check**

In most respects this is a very well-behaved cultivar. Where growing conditions make it vulnerable, downy mildew can affect it in the first half of the season.

**Garden Uses**

One to be put into mixed schemes and mixed borders or grown on its own.

### OVERALL ASSESSMENT ★★★★

✔ One of the most beautiful to look at.

✖ Needs a location and growing method that will not encourage downy mildew.

# Escapade

## Bush Rose (Floribunda)

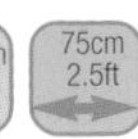

zone 7

### FLOWER PROPERTIES ★★★★

**Colour**

A mixture of rose pink, blended with warm lilac and white. The warm lilac pink is arranged around the outer edge of the flower, and the contrasting pure white is at the centre. In hotter conditions the pink becomes deeper as the flower ages.

**Size and Shape**

The buds are small, fresh and light green. They open slowly at first, revealing the deeper colour. Blooms become fully open imperceptibly, their 15 petals showing off their innocent beauty. At up to 9cm (3.5in) across, these flowers delight the most demanding observer.

**Scent**

Fresh and sweet, with a traditional rose perfume.

**Production**

Flowers are produced with generosity. Clusters of up to 15 blooms keep the plant in full flower for weeks. This rose is very reliable at producing a good display late in the season. A lot of flower for the space used in the garden.

### PLANT PROPERTIES ★★★

**Shape and Size**

A slightly more upright plant than average. The bush will be around 1.2m (4ft) tall but no more than 75cm (2ft 6in) wide.

**Position**

An easy-to-grow garden plant, content in all but shady sites.

**Hardiness**

A cultivar that will not enjoy the coldest regions.

### FOLIAGE PROPERTIES ★★★★

**Colour**

Leaves are in the paler range of green with a matt sheen. They are fairly large but slightly more slender than average. Foliage cover is reasonable but not one of the most dense.

**Health Check**

A tendency to contract blackspot in the late season, but good tolerance to other malaises.

**Garden Uses**

Mixed with other species in a border or used on its own, it is a worthy addition to any planting scheme.

### OVERALL ASSESSMENT ★★★★

- ✔ The enchanting beauty and innocence that it portrays.
- ✖ The plant is slightly upright and tends to become a little bare on the lower half, leaving too much stem on display.

# Fellowship

## Bush Rose (Floribunda)

  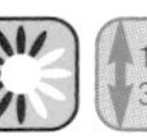 

### FLOWER PROPERTIES ★★★★★

**Colour**

A strong, deep, burnished orange. When the sun shines on it there is an iridescent quality, surprising in such a deep colour. One of the strengths of this cultivar is its ability to keep the colour throughout the life of the flower. Come sun or rain, there is no noticeable fading or deterioration.

**Size and Shape**

Opening from mid-green buds, the flower starts life as a pointed orange bud, from which petals unfurl. As it opens, the flower transforms to a perfect circle with the petals in the centre arching inwards. With 30 petals and a flower averaging 9cm (3.5in) across, we are delighted with a flower showing us beauty through all stages.

**Scent**

The distinct scent has traces of spice and myrrh.

**Production**

Clusters form in groups of five to seven blooms. They are very quick to repeat, giving an extended flowering period. Flowers are produced all over the top of the bush, providing maximum impact.

### PLANT PROPERTIES ★★★★★

**Shape and Size**

This is a plant that always looks right. There are plenty of stems, all growing to an even and regular pattern. Bushes are compact, strong and dense. As a mature plant it will be no more than 1.1m (3ft 6in) tall and 75cm (2ft 6in) wide.

**Position**

In all garden positions except shaded areas.

**Hardiness**

A tough cultivar, and one that is worth trying even in the most demanding locations.

### FOLIAGE PROPERTIES ★★★★

**Colour**

Mid- to dark green with a deep shine. The leaves are large, exuding a willingness to perform. They are numerous on the plant, contributing to its appearance of vitality.

**Health Check**

A healthy variety, which will give few problems. In adverse conditions it may suffer from a mild dose of either downy mildew or blackspot, but not enough to damage the plant.

**Garden Uses**

It will flourish in any garden situation.

### OVERALL ASSESSMENT ★★★★

✔ The robust willingness to perform. Masses of colour.

✖ The colour is strong and is not the easiest to combine in mixed plantings.

# Greetings

## Bush Rose (Floribunda)

1m 3ft

### FLOWER PROPERTIES ★★★★

**Colour**

Purple colours with random splashes of white near the centre of the petals. A very stable colour in all weather, which is rare for this shade.

**Size and Shape**

The flowers are only 5cm (2in) across and have 25 petals. They open quickly to be fairly flat and then stay that way, smiling up at all who look at them.

**Scent**

There is a distinct scent with a hint of aniseed.

**Production**

Clusters can have up to 25 buds opening over a long period. The plant will be buried under its own display of flowers, and there is an equally strong performance late in the season.

### PLANT PROPERTIES ★★★★

**Shape and Size**

Below average height and bushy. No more than 1m (3ft) tall and 60cm (2ft) wide .

**Position**

Great in beds and borders.

**Hardiness**

A strong rose, which will perform well in all conditions.

### FOLIAGE PROPERTIES ★★★★

**Colour**

Foliage is good, with a deep lustre and a rich emerald colour. With plenty to cover the plant, the leaves act as a pretty foil to the deep flower colour.

**Health Check**

Adequate in most areas. Some powdery mildew may occur in the second half of the season.

**Garden Uses**

Use in beds, borders and garden tubs.

### OVERALL ASSESSMENT ★★★

✔ A great deep colour which is stable in sun.

✖ It lacks the strength of character that makes a great rose.

# Iceberg

## Bush Rose (Floribunda)

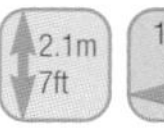

FLOWER PROPERTIES ★★★★★

**Colour**

It is good to have a colour that is easy to describe and one in which there is very little room for different interpretations: it is white. That sounds simple, until you realize how many different whites there are. This is the white of a fluffy cumulus cloud on a sunny day. It may take a light pink hue on some occasions.

**Size and Shape**

The buds are small and light green, opening to flowers of 6cm (2.5in) wide or a little smaller in very hot conditions. Petals are shorter in the centre of the bloom, giving a flat flower with 25 petals.

**Scent**

The best description of the scent is 'absent'.

**Production**

Its strongest suit. Clusters of buds are massive and plentiful, opening over a few weeks. During that time there will be a sea of white flowers. With a quick cycle that allows it to repeat bloom, this rose gives a prodigious quantity of flowers in the season.

PLANT PROPERTIES ★★★★

**Shape and Size**

The shape of the mature plant is lovely. It grows into a large rounded bush, always even and with good growth low down. At 1.2–2.2m (4–7ft) tall and 1–1.5m (3–5ft) wide, this is a substantial garden rose.

**Position**

Grow in any position with good levels of light.

**Hardiness**

In spite of its slightly tender appearance, it is, in fact, hardy in all but the coldest regions.

FOLIAGE PROPERTIES ★★★

**Colour**

Light green leaf with a promising shine to it. Leaves are a little on the small side and spread too thinly over the plant. The overall effect is that the plant looks sparse.

**Health Check**

Susceptible to powdery mildew. In poor conditions downy mildew may also be a problem.

**Garden Uses**

Grow as an individual specimen in a hedge or in mixed borders.

OVERALL ASSESSMENT ★★★★

✔ The purity of the white and the divine plant shape.

✖ The foliage lets it down: it is not entirely healthy and a little sparse.

# L'Aimant

## Bush Rose (Floribunda)

FLOWER PROPERTIES ★★★★★

**Colour**

Rose pink with the subtlest tones of peach lightly added. The colour fades as the flower ages, and it may benefit from deadheading before the petals fall naturally.

**Size and Shape**

Well-rounded buds. The early flower shape has a long petal in bud form, opening to many shorter petals curling around the flower centre. An attractive flower shape containing 50 petals in blooms often 8cm (3in) across.

**Scent**

This has to be one of the best. A complex blend of the finest rose scents, strong and addictively intoxicating.

**Production**

The clusters of flower are usually no more than five buds. The centre bloom is always the largest, but all are attractive. This cultivar begins to flower earlier in the season than average and repeats well throughout.

PLANT PROPERTIES ★★★★

**Shape and Size**

A strong and compact plant that consists of plenty of shoots from the base. When mature it will be 1m (3ft) tall and just over 60cm (2ft) wide.

**Position**

It is able to adapt to any open position. Partial sunlight is acceptable

**Hardiness**

A strong cultivar suited to all regions.

FOLIAGE PROPERTIES ★★★

**Colour**

There is plenty of foliage to make the plant look robust and lush. The leaves are fairly dark and, allied to a good shine, give an attractive effect.

**Health Check**

The main bugbear is a susceptibility to blackspot. Grow in good conditions to reduce the chance of an attack.

**Garden Uses**

A valuable addition to borders or beds. Remember to plant where the perfume can be appreciated.

OVERALL ASSESSMENT ★★★★

✔ One of the best perfumes you can enjoy. Good as a cut flower.

✖ The flower can fade. Plant not absolutely healthy.

# *Louisa Stone*

## Bush Rose (Floribunda)

FLOWER PROPERTIES ★★★★

**Colour**

An intricate blend of off-white to honey. The deeper shades are towards the centre of the flower; there is a subtle gradation to the paler shades. The flower opens well in all but the wettest conditions.

**Size and Shape**

Round buds open to young flowers that start life as a pointed bud. This quickly changes to become a flower with complex and intricate arrangements of petals . With 40 petals, and a diameter of 8cm (3in) when fully open, there is beauty at every stage of the flower's development.

**Scent**

Blessed with a pleasing perfume that has hints of apple and rose.

**Production**

Clusters average five blooms, and there are usually plenty of them, making this a very productive and colourful garden plant. There is a short interlude between flushes of flower.

PLANT PROPERTIES ★★★★

**Shape and size**

Below average size and with stems that can be a little on the lax side, this creates a thick, dense plant, with a shape that is closer to dome than upright. A mature plant will grow no more than 1m (3ft) tall and around 75cm (2ft 6in) wide.

**Position**

Gives good results in all but the shadiest parts of the garden.

**Hardiness**

Will survive in colder regions if protected. Happy in hot regions.

FOLIAGE PROPERTIES

**Colour** ★★★★★

Dark green with a slight bronze hue and very glossy. The leaves are large and there are lots of them. One of the leafier roses – the entire bush is well furnished with foliage from top to bottom.

**Health Check**

Resilient and reluctant to succumb to ailments. There may be minor problems with blackspot at the end of the season.

**Garden Uses**

Mixed borders or beds or large patio planters.

OVERALL ASSESSMENT ★★★★

✔ Overall impression of vitality and well-being from leaf and flower.

✖ The lax stems can bend too much if the flowers are heavy or loaded with rain.

# *Margaret Merril*
## Bush Rose (Floribunda)

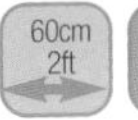

### FLOWER PROPERTIES ★★★★

**Colour**

The overall impression is white, but it is not a pure white. The flower has a pearly pink centre in the early stages of development. The intensity of the pink coloration varies from year to year, depending on the conditions that season. As the flower opens fully, the pink disperses and the white dominates. Very good resistance to weather damage: heavy rain makes insignificant blemishes.

**Size and Shape**

A rare treat is in store with this rose. There are three distinct stages to the flower, and each is beautiful. It starts with an elegant pointed bud, ideal for cutting. At the second stage the pointed centre remains but is surrounded by circles of perfect petals. Finally, the centre opens to reveal a pretty flower proudly showing off its stamens. All this is achieved from no more than 25 petals.

**Scent**

If I like the flower, it is nothing compared to the scent. Sweet rose and so strong it must be in the top ten.

**Production**

Produced in small clusters, the plant has an adequate supply of flowers, but it is not a cultivar that covers every square inch with bloom. It repeats well in the late season.

### PLANT PROPERTIES ★★★

**Shape and Size**

Bushes grow well but do not willingly produce masses of new basal canes. This leads them to be more upright than average. The average height will be 1.1m (3ft 6in) and a little over 60cm (2ft) wide.

**Position**

Best to avoid heavy shade as that will accentuate its tendency to grow up rather than out.

**Hardiness**

Quite hardy but not perfect. Protect well in the coldest regions.

### FOLIAGE PROPERTIES ★★★★★

**Colour**

The leaves are dark green with a good lustre to them. They are spaced out too much on the plant, so it will never look fully clad. If it is allowed to grow too tall and leggy, the bottom of the plant will be bereft of foliage.

**Health Check**

Blackspot is likely with this cultivar. Work on the assumption that prevention is better than cure.

**Garden Uses**

To provide the most wonderful cut flowers and in mixed beds or borders.

### OVERALL ASSESSMENT ★★★★

✔ If you appreciate beauty in a flower and perfume, it is a must-have.

✖ If you appreciate the easy life, this rose is too much work to keep in good condition.

# Mountbatten

## Bush Rose (Floribunda)

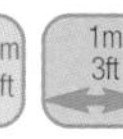

zone 6–7

### FLOWER PROPERTIES ★★★★

**Colour**

The main colour is a deep mimosa yellow. This sometimes, but not always, adopts a pink flush as the flower ages. Firm petals give excellent resistance to damage from wind and rain.

**Size and Shape**

The bud is well rounded and full of promise. Initially it is a high-centred flower; as the bloom develops it opens to a wide flower, with shorter petals in the centre. These will continue to arch towards the centre. With over 45 petals and often 9cm (3.5in) across, it is a long-lasting pleasurable flower.

**Scent**

In the middle range as far as strength is concerned, featuring lemon, musk and honey aromas.

**Production**

The clusters are small, often no more than five buds to each. The flowers are held above the foliage on strong stems, and there are plenty of them, both for early- and late-season flowering.

### PLANT PROPERTIES ★★★★

**Shape and Size**

A cultivar that obviously enjoys growing. The plant is strong, bushy and robust, with plentiful strong basal shoots, making a vibrant bush to 1.4m (4.5ft) tall and 1m (3ft) across.

**Position**

It is happy in most situations, including light shade. Avoid planting in darker areas.

**Hardiness**

Although it is tough, in the coldest areas it will struggle unless given some protection.

### FOLIAGE PROPERTIES ★★★★

**Colour**

Prolific quantities of leaves are produced, which add to the vitality of the plant. They are nicely glossed, dark green and with definite serration around the edges.

**Health Check**

When the plant is kept in good conditions it will reward you with exemplary behaviour. When it is under stress blackspot may occur.

**Garden Uses**

Formal rose gardens or beds or mixed borders.

### OVERALL ASSESSMENT ★★★★

✔ An able performer in all areas. The contrast between flower and leaf is successful.

✖ While it is adequate in all respects, it excels in none – a few more flowers would swing the balance.

# Oranges and Lemons
## Bush Rose (Floribunda)

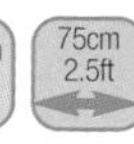

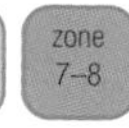


zone 7–8

### FLOWER PROPERTIES ★★★★

**Colour**

There are two colours in this striped beauty, as the name implies. Orange is the basic flower colour, with yellow added generously in bold stripes. It makes a flamboyant display in a vase or massed on the plant.

**Size and Shape**

Unlike many other novelty cultivars there is no loss of flower size or form. Opening to be 9cm (3.5in) across and constructed of around 30 petals, the flower has plenty of substance to enhance its flamboyance.

**Scent**

There is a light scent, very much a secondary feature compared to the visual interest.

**Production**

This cultivar has the ability to generate copious quantities of flowers. They come in clusters, neatly arranged above the foliage and in the ideal position to exhibit their exotic colours. Quick to repeat bloom into the late season.

### PLANT PROPERTIES ★★★★

**Shape and Size**

A willing performer that matures into a bushy plant. A satisfactory supply of basal shoots produces a plant of 1.1m (3ft 6in) tall and 75cm (2ft 6in) wide.

**Position**

Good in sunny positions or light shade. Avoid medium to heavy shade.

**Hardiness**

Reasonable but not perfect. Difficult in colder regions.

### FOLIAGE PROPERTIES ★★★★

**Colour**

There is a lot of leaf on the plant. Leaves are large, lush and closely spaced. Starting a pleasing shade of red and developing to dark green, they exude a sense of vitality.

**Health Check**

Provide good growing conditions and there will be little trouble. It can suffer from downy mildew or blackspot in adverse conditions.

**Garden Uses**

Somewhere in the spotlight to show off its extravagant colour scheme.

### OVERALL ASSESSMENT ★★★★

✔ A fine constitution for such a showy colour.

✖ Better as an individual rather than in mixed planting schemes.

# Pink Abundance

## Bush Rose (Floribunda)

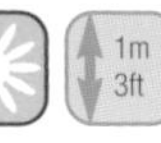

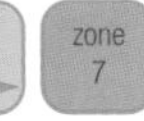


zone 7

### FLOWER PROPERTIES ★★★★

**Colour**

Deep rose-pink flowers. The colour is warm, glowing in the sunshine and brightening a dull day. It is well behaved in nearly all weather conditions, although very strong sunshine can cause it to fade to a less attractive bluish-pink. If this happens, just deadhead and enjoy the remaining flowers.

**Size and Shape**

Round buds open to provide flowers that retain a cupped shape, with petals that reflex to the centre. They will never be large blooms – no more than 5cm (2in) across – with 35 petals.

**Scent**

A light musk and lemon perfume.

**Production**

Many trusses of flowers are produced, with the buds close together in the truss. As the flowers open they will touch, giving complete coverage. Flowers continue to open in the truss for many days. With its admirably ability to repeat quickly, this cultivar has a long flowering season.

### PLANT PROPERTIES ★★★

**Shape and Size**

Shorter than average, but it produces an almost continuous supply of flowering stems. Compact and bushy, growing no more than 1m (3ft) tall by 75cm (2ft 6in) wide.

**Position**

Best in a reasonably open position, not too shady.

**Hardiness**

A strong plant, but it will not enjoy the coldest areas.

### FOLIAGE PROPERTIES ★★★

**Colour**

Copious foliage: dark, shiny leaves are crammed on to the stems, so the plant will look solid and full of leaf.

**Health Check**

Reliable but not perfect. Under stress it is susceptible to downy mildew or blackspot.

**Garden Uses**

In beds and rose gardens or anywhere you need a splash of colour.

### OVERALL ASSESSMENT ★★★★

✔ The quantity of flower makes this one of the best.

✖ Watch it carefully to spot trouble and act immediately to keep it healthy.

# Princess of Wales

## Bush Rose (Floribunda)

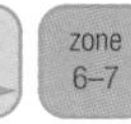


zone 6–7

### FLOWER PROPERTIES ★★★★★

**Colour**

White: a bright clean white that will almost dazzle in strong sunlight. On rare occasions it may have a slight pink flush. For a white flower it resists rain damage well.

**Size and Shape**

The buds are round, opening to show a white, conical flower, the outer petals wrapping around the others as if protecting them. Inner petals are shorter than the outer, so as it opens the final result is a flat flower with several rows of petals neatly arranged on top of each other. Each flower is 6cm (2.5in) wide with 35 petals.

**Scent**

There is a gentle suggestion of rose and myrrh.

**Production**

Top marks are awarded here. The clusters are long lasting, with an average of nine buds, which open in an orderly sequence. No sooner is one cluster over than the next is racing to take its place. Be disappointed if you don't get three flushes of flower in a season.

### PLANT PROPERTIES ★★★

**Shape and Size**

A desirable growing habit. The bush generates plenty of growth, but it is controlled, forming a plant that is even in appearance and rounded in shape. The benefit of a rounded shape is that it allows flowers to be produced close to ground level. This rose flowers from just above ground to the top; it is only about 75cm (2ft 6in) tall and 60cm (2ft) wide.

**Position**

Does best in positions with reasonable light, but it tolerates shade as well.

**Hardiness**

Give protection in the harshest regions and it will survive.

### FOLIAGE PROPERTIES ★★★★★

**Colour**

The leaves are mid-green, large and numerous. The plant will be fully covered, with no gaps. The leaves have an understated look of durability to them, not glossy but with a rich patina.

**Health Check**

Excellent at repelling ailments. The only slip-up is the occasional outbreak of downy mildew.

**Garden Uses**

In patio planters, beds and borders. White always improves a mixed colour scheme.

### OVERALL ASSESSMENT ★★★★

✔ Purity of the colour and copious flower production.

✖ Individual flowers could last a bit longer.

# Purple Tiger
## Bush Rose (Floribunda)

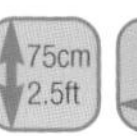

zone 7–8

### FLOWER PROPERTIES ★★★

**Colour**

If you like something a little different this rose may suit you. The flower is decorated in radial stripes of purple and white. It may sound vulgar, but it is both unusual and engaging.

**Size and Shape**

These flowers will never be big – expect no more than 6cm (2in 6in) across. With 25 petals, the flower opens flat, which is the best shape to show off its stripes.

**Scent**

Enjoy a hint of spice and rose; pleasing without being strong.

**Production**

Flowers in clusters that are held prettily above the foliage, each cluster of up to 12 buds. The flowering is quick to repeat, so you don't have to wait long to decide whether you still like this eccentric flower.

### PLANT PROPERTIES ★★★

**Shape and Size**

A short plant that will not often grow above 75cm (2ft 6in) tall, it is reasonably bushy (growing to 60cm (2ft) wide.

**Position**

Plant somewhere where it will get a good amount of sun.

**Hardiness**

Best to avoid the coldest regions.

### FOLIAGE PROPERTIES ★★★

**Colour**

Leaves are a light green and a little more sparse on the plant than is desirable.

**Health Check**

For a rose with novelty flowers, the health is good. Keep the growing conditions optimum to retain health.

**Garden Uses**

Mixed borders or somewhere where you want the eccentric.

### OVERALL ASSESSMENT ★★★★

✔ The unusual flower.

✖ The foliage and plant are not up to a very high standard.

# Remembrance

## Bush Rose (Floribunda)

zone 6–7

### FLOWER PROPERTIES ★★★★★

**Colour**

An iridescent bright scarlet, almost as bright as a field of poppies. The flowers are impervious to the effects of either a burning sun or a heavy storm.

**Size and Shape**

The flowers pop out of rounded buds, mimicking the shape of the bud in the early stages. Rounded blooms show the reverse of the outer petals. The inner rows of petals mass prettily together in circular rows. With 45 petals and at no more than 6cm (2.5in) across, there are many petals packed into the flower.

**Scent**

This rose is all show – a show to see, however, and not to smell.

**Production**

It would be unreasonable to fault it. Produces abundant, well-spaced clusters to cover the surface of the plant and there open over a long period, extending the flowering to the maximum. Then it has the audacity to repeat bloom and do it all again.

### PLANT PROPERTIES ★★★★

**Shape and Size**

Makes a framework of shoots that allow a rounded shape to develop as the plant matures. It will never become very tall, probably no more than 75cm (2ft 6in), with a girth of 60cm (2ft).

**Position**

A truly utilitarian rose for every position.

**Hardiness**

With protection in the coldest areas it should survive. It will be happy elsewhere.

### FOLIAGE PROPERTIES ★★★★

**Colour**

Small leaves, with lots of serrations round the edges. Emerald green in colour, having a polish that would be the envy of any cabinet-maker. The leaves are close to each other on the stem, covering the whole plant.

**Health Check**

When under stress downy mildew may attack. Other problems will be negligible.

**Garden Uses**

Beds, borders and low hedges. Anywhere for a stunning impact.

### OVERALL ASSESSMENT ★★★★

- ✔ A colourful flower on a manageable, well-behaved plant.
- ✖ Grow in good conditions or downy mildew will be a problem.

# Scentimental
## Bush Rose (Floribunda)

   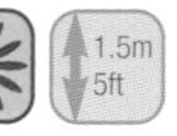

### FLOWER PROPERTIES ★★★★★

**Colour**

Two distinct colours make a dramatic statement. Claret red predominates, with stripes and splashes of white all over. Unlike many bicolour roses, this one retains a clear definition of its two colours until the petals fall. The intricate colour patterns are undamaged by rain or strong sunshine.

**Size and Shape**

The buds are medium size and start with a delectable pointed centre. As they develop further, the large petals open to show off a bloom fully 8cm (3in) across with up to 30 petals.

**Scent**

The perfume is a strong, sweet, spicy combination, which infuses the area around the plant.

**Production**

Many novelty cultivars are reluctant to bloom freely. This is an exception, providing fine clusters in generous quantities, enough to cover the plant in blooms in the early season. With strong late-season blooming as well, there are months of pleasure to enjoy.

### PLANT PROPERTIES ★★★

**Shape and Size**

Its habit of branching out from the base in a profligate manner guarantees a bushy plant. Strong stems ensure that the flowers are held upright as the plant grows to between 1 and 1.5m (3–5ft) tall. Expect it to be in the region of 75cm–1.1m (2ft 6in–3ft 6in) wide

**Position**

A quality performer in all but the shadiest spots of the garden.

**Hardiness**

Protection is required in the coldest regions, otherwise it will be happy.

### FOLIAGE PROPERTIES ★★★★★

**Colour**

Luxuriant dark green leaves give the plant an aura of success. Not only are the leaves large, they are closely packed along the stem, making the plant attractive even before it blooms.

**Health Check**

As long as the plant is not growing under stress, it will be trouble free. In adverse conditions it can be mildly susceptible to blackspot

**Garden Uses**

Plant it where it can show off its extrovert flowers.

### OVERALL ASSESSMENT ★★★★

✔ A novelty flower on a very fine plant.

✖ It may get just a bit bigger than we would like.

# Sexy Rexy

## Bush Rose (Floribunda)

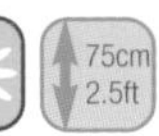

### FLOWER PROPERTIES ★★★★★

**Colour**

A bright and iridescent rose pink. The buds are a slightly deeper shade when first open. Retains its colour well and is able withstand a beating from wind and rain without appreciable damage.

**Size and Shape**

Not the largest of flowers, only to 8cm (3in) across, in spite of having at least 40 petals each. Buds will be rounded and plump. With short petals in the centre of the flowers they develop into an open bloom with a low flower centre crowded with petals.

**Scent**

A variety that provides a visual display not an aromatic experience.

**Production**

There can be few rivals in the competition to provide most flowers. Clusters abound, with each containing up to 45 buds. As the flowers open in sequence, the display is both dense and long lasting. This performance will be repeated later in the season.

### PLANT PROPERTIES ★★★

**Shape and Size**

Short, compact and dense in its growing habit. Makes lots of basal growth and benefits from hard pruning. In very windy sites the weight of the flowers can be too much for the stems to hold upright. In most gardens expect a height of 75cm (2ft 6in) tall and 60cm (2ft) wide.

**Position**

Will thrive in any open position if not too windy. Partial sunlight is acceptable

**Hardiness**

Survives well in most regions.

### FOLIAGE PROPERTIES ★★★★★

**Colour**

One of the additional beauties is the rich purple of the young foliage. It soon changes to green with bronze undertones.

**Health Check**

In very dry, hot summers there may be some powdery mildew. Overall, the health is good: keep the plant happy and it will reward you by staying healthy.

**Garden Uses**

Anywhere, from mixed borders to formal rose gardens.

### OVERALL ASSESSMENT ★★★★

✔ The colour and ease of management in the garden.

✖ Needs correct location – avoid anywhere very windy or sunny.

# Simply the Best
## Bush Rose (Floribunda)

   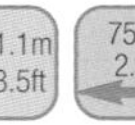 

**FLOWER PROPERTIES** ★★★★

**Colour**
Amber, peach and pink combinations. The deeper and pink shades increase as the flower ages in hot sunshine. Withstands rain damage.

**Size and Shape**
The flowers are a good size but are not large. With over 50 petals arranged in neat patterns and swirls, the 6cm (2.5in) blooms are packed with interest.

**Scent**
Light and pleasing, with a hint of citronella.

**Production**
Numerous, long-lasting flowers give a dense display in both early and late season.

**PLANT PROPERTIES**

**Shape and Size** ★★★★
This plant is eager to grow, producing basal shoots that are strong and frequent. It is bushy and retains an even shape. Growing to 1.1m (3ft 6in) tall and 75cm (2ft 6in) wide, it makes a perfect garden plant.

**Position**
Will thrive in any open position. Partial sunlight is acceptable.

**Hardiness**
It may not enjoy the coldest regions.

**FOLIAGE PROPERTIES**

**Colour** ★★★★
The foliage is dark and exudes vigour. There is plenty of it on all the stems so that the plant is well furnished from tip to toe.

**Health Check**
When it is growing in good conditions there will be few problems.

**Garden Uses**
An asset in any garden situation.

**OVERALL ASSESSMENT**

✔ An excellent performer, combining a good flowering ability with abundant, luxuriant foliage. ★★★★

✖ A slightly more definite colour would be an improvement.

# bush roses
# hybrid tea

# Big Purple

## Bush Rose (Hybrid Tea)

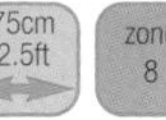


zone 8

### FLOWER PROPERTIES ★★★★

**Colour**

The name is a bit of a giveaway. This is a deep red that has purple as a dominant tone. In the young flower it is very attractive, but as the flower ages the colour loses its beauty. Deadhead to keep it looking tidy.

**Size and Shape**

Another giveaway: it is big. With 45 petals and developing to 13cm (5in) across, this is a monster of a flower. The shape is all that you could desire from a large-flowered hybrid tea.

**Scent**

A strong, sweet rose experience that you are sure to enjoy.

**Production**

One of the weaker points – there will never be really dense flower cover. Adequate in the first flush but light in the late blooming.

### PLANT PROPERTIES ★★★

**Shape and Size**

The plant is tall, growing to 1.4m (4ft 6in) and 75cm (2ft 6in) wide. It will tend to become a little leggy, with bare stems on the lower parts of the plant.

**Position**

Give it sun, but not too much intense midday sun.

**Hardiness**

Not suitable for very cold areas or windy sites.

### FOLIAGE PROPERTIES ★★★★★

**Colour**

The leaves are big, but the colour is a slightly dull grey-green. They may be absent on the lower reaches of a mature plant.

**Health Check**

Keep your eye open for ailments and act quickly to stop them spreading. Mildew and blackspot will attack a stressed plant.

**Garden Uses**

Rose beds and borders.

### OVERALL ASSESSMENT ★★★★

✔ The outstanding colour and good perfume.

✖ Not healthy enough to be a trouble-free pleasure.

# Elina

## Bush Rose (Hybrid Tea)

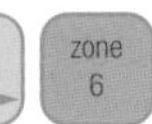


### FLOWER PROPERTIES ★★★★

**Colour**

This is a pale rose, ranging from almost white to lemon sorbet. The deeper colouring is in the centre of the flower. Unlike many pale-coloured cultivars this is a good performer in all weathers: hot, cold or wet, the flower is clean and fresh.

**Size and Shape**

It is obvious from the appearance of the buds, which are large and pointed, that we are about to enjoy a large flower. Initially, the petals intertwine into a classic long-pointed bud. As it opens the flower becomes more rounded, but spectacular – often more than 13cm (5 in) across with 45 petals.

**Scent**

There are many good aspects to this rose, but it is lacking in perfume.

**Production**

Considering the sheer size of the flowers, it is able to produce a prodigious quantity in a season. Repeat flowering keeps the flowers going until late. The long, straight stems make them good for cutting.

### PLANT PROPERTIES ★★★

**Shape and Size**

The bush matches the flower: it is big, strong and bold, with plenty of strong growth from the base. Expect it to be between 1.2 and 1.8m (4–6ft) tall and to extend between 75cm and 1.1m (2ft 6in–3ft 6in) wide.

**Position**

Good for borders or beds where height is required.

**Hardiness**

Just as you would expect from such a strong grower, it is happy to thrive in all areas.

### FOLIAGE PROPERTIES ★★★★★

**Colour**

To match the plant and flowers, it produces big, strong leaves. They are dark green, and there are lots of them, covering the substantial plant. They are absolutely in keeping with the other features of the rose.

**Health Check**

A fine reputation for having a robust constitution that will repel any attacks to its health. In good conditions it will remain completely healthy.

**Garden Uses**

In a hedge or bed as a feature.

### OVERALL ASSESSMENT ★★★★

✔ Tough and easy, with robust health. It will keep its leaves through a mild winter.

✖ Flowers tend to sit near the top on long stems, leaving lots of plant below.

# Ingrid Bergman

## Bush Rose (Hybrid Tea)

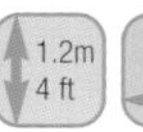

### FLOWER PROPERTIES ★★★★★

**Colour**

Here we have the colour that epitomizes love: a deep red with an almost velvet property. How we love to give or receive a dozen of these red roses. The colour is stable, fading only in hot climates. It can suffer some spotting in wet conditions

**Size and Shape**

Large and bold without being vulgar. The bud is pointed and retains its classic shape for several days. With 45 large petals, it takes a few days to develop into a fully open bloom, which can be more than 10cm (4in) across.

**Scent**

There is a haunting sweetness to the perfume.

**Production**

The flowers usually come as large individuals. Where they appear in clusters the first flower is the major event, the others will be smaller and in the role of a supporting act, but still lovely. With a good ability to repeat bloom, this rose gives pleasure for a long time every year, both in the garden and as a cut flower.

### PLANT PROPERTIES ★★★★

**Shape and Size**

A strong growing plant that produces plenty of thick canes from the base. It acquires a bushy habit as it matures to about 1.2m (4ft) tall and 75cm (2ft 6in) wide.

**Position**

Avoid the extremes of intensely sunny positions or heavy shade.

**Hardiness**

It may look tough, but it will not enjoy life in very cold areas.

### FOLIAGE PROPERTIES ★★★

**Colour**

Starting out red and turning to dark green, the leaves are robust and plentiful, having all the visual qualities to match the strengths of the plant.

**Health Check**

No troubles early in the season. Later it can suffer from some blackspot.

**Garden Uses**

A fine rose to use in beds, on its own or in mixed plantings.

### OVERALL ASSESSMENT ★★★★

✔ An arresting and seductive colour allied to a distinguished perfume.

✖ Can be a bit fussy, and it will perform much better in its ideal conditions.

# *Just Joey*

## Bush Rose (Hybrid Tea)

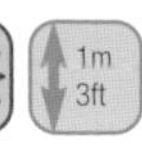

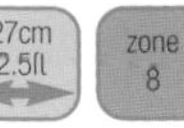


zone 8

### FLOWER PROPERTIES ★★★★

**Colour**

In ideal conditions there are few better colours. Blend copper and peach together to picture this rose's warm tone. Unfortunately, in hot regions the colour will be less awe inspiring, becoming pale and washed out.

**Size and Shape**

Tall buds open with long petals. The flower evolves into wide cupped blooms; the large petals are curved and elegant with scalloped edges. There never seem to be enough petals – about 30 in all – but it doesn't matter. The flower is large, 11cm (4.5in) across and is beautiful none the less.

**Scent**

Strong, with the sweetness of a favourite rose perfume.

**Production**

A cultivar that provides some of the earliest flowers of the season. Borne in small clusters, with the first bloom having greater stature than the others, the early flowering is spectacular. Strong autumn flowering follows.

### PLANT PROPERTIES ★★★

**Shape and Size**

Do not expect anything too big. This plant will be no more than 1m (3ft) tall. It grows branches that spread out wide, so in spite of the low height it will still be up to 75cm (2ft 6in) wide. There are not quite enough stems to make a dense bush, and it often looks a little sparse.

**Position**

Grow in good conditions. Do not plant in heavy to medium shade.

**Hardiness**

This is not the hardiest rose and will not thrive in very cold regions.

### FOLIAGE PROPERTIES ★★★

**Colour**

The leaves have a pleasing appearance. Their colour is deep and reassuring, and the upper surface greets you with a deep shine. Although they are large, they are spaced out on the stem so the plant looks a little bare.

**Health Check**

Imperfections are not always disastrous, and the likelihood is that powdery mildew and blackspot will attack in the late season. Both can be controlled with good culture and careful management of the plant.

**Garden Uses**

In rose beds and mixed borders.

### OVERALL ASSESSMENT ★★★★

✔ The flower is too lovely to be ignored.

✖ The plant is not as lovely as the flower and requires work to get the best from it.

# Marilyn Monroe

## Bush Rose (Hybrid Tea)

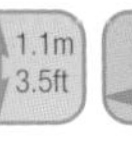

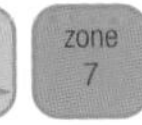


### FLOWER PROPERTIES ★★★★★

**Colour**

A blend of apricot and cream that is so gorgeous it looks edible. The pale shades round the outside of the bloom blend irresistibly with the richer apricots of the flower centre. The intensity of colour at the flower centre draws our attention away from the soft outer areas of the flower. In spite of this soft and gentle appearance, the flowers are robust, with firm petals that resist damage from rain with ease. In very sunny conditions the outer petals will begin to fade but will not burn or scorch.

**Size and Shape**

The petals swirl and curl into the prettiest hybrid tea shape. With 30 petals to each flower there is plenty of substance to keep the shape for several days. Expect it to open to 9cm (3.5in) across when mature.

**Scent**

There is a light and mild fresh perfume that is neither absent nor overwhelming.

**Production**

Small clusters of no more than five buds with an abundance of shapely flowers in both early and late season. The flowers are always produced on long stems, which keep the blooms looking upwards.

★★★

### PLANT PROPERTIES

**Shape and Size**

A well-behaved plant that grows to around 1.1m (3ft 6in) tall and 75cm (2ft 6in) wide. The shape is neat and even, and flowers are held proudly over the rounded bush.

**Position**

A good performance in all areas; it is especially fond of hot weather and will flourish in full sunlight.

**Hardiness**

Survives well in most regions but it is best to avoid areas of low light. ★★★★★

### FOLIAGE PROPERTIES

**Colour**

One of the additional beauties is the rich purple of the young foliage. It soon changes to green with bronze undertones.

**Health Check**

In very dry, hot summers there may be some powdery mildew but that should be your only concern. Overall, the health is good, and if you keep the plant happy it will reward you.

**Garden Uses**

This rose will flourish anywhere, from mixed borders to formal rose gardens. ★★★

### OVERALL ASSESSMENT

✔ The colour and shape of the flowers.

✖ It could produce a few more flowers.

# New Zealand

## Bush Rose (Hybrid Tea)

zone 7–8

FLOWER PROPERTIES ★★★★

**Colour**

This is a pale pink, deepening towards the outside of the flower. It is not the most inspiring colour and may best be described as gentle and soft. Rain can cause some discoloration to the soft petals.

**Size and Shape**

Produces big flowers although each has only 35 petals. All the flowers will be the same: large, high-pointed centres in the classic form, reaching 10cm (4in) across.

**Scent**

The real reason to grow this rose is its perfume. It is almost too strong to be real, but too beautiful to be artificial.

**Production**

The large flowers will be single blooms or in small clusters. In clusters there will be only one large flower and three or four smaller blooms. Producing a respectable volume of flowers in both early and late season, it will satisfy without excelling.

PLANT PROPERTIES ★★★

**Shape and Size**

The plant is more upright than average, maturing to 1.1m (3ft 6in) tall and 75cm (2ft 6in) wide. It branches from the base, which helps to maintain a strong and virile plant.

**Position**

Needs reasonable light. Any areas of heavy shade should be avoided.

**Hardiness**

Will not survive in cold regions without thorough protection.

FOLIAGE PROPERTIES ★★★★★

**Colour**

Leaves are big and bold, growing in good quantity from the top to low down on the plant. They inspire confidence with their rich green colour and lacquered shine.

**Health Check**

Health is unexpectedly good, resisting most attempted infections. There can be some powdery mildew late in the season.

**Garden Uses**

In rose beds and borders, where the scent can be enjoyed.

OVERALL ASSESSMENT ★★★★

✔ Perfume and good overall behaviour.

✖ The colour could be more inspirational. A little light in flower production.

# Paul Shirville

## Bush Rose (Hybrid Tea)

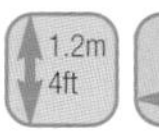

### LOWER PROPERTIES ★★★★★

**Colour**

At first glance the eye sees a pink rose, verging on salmon pink. Looking more deeply into the flower we pick up a complex blend of colours, ranging from a dash of yellow, through a spectrum of pinks to the salmon pinks. It is the way the colours mix together that produces the final result – one from which the colour positively radiates out.

**Size and Shape**

The formation of the flower is exquisite at all stages. Starting with a high-centred bud, the petals curl seductively round, forming an elegant point. The flower can open to be more than 9cm (3.5 in) wide and still maintain a pointed centre with its petals reflexing enticingly.

**Scent**

The perfume is a classic rose scent.

**Production**

Produced either as single blooms or in groups of up to five, there will be plenty on the plant to make a strong display. It is able to produce repeat blooms throughout the season. Cut them for the house to encourage the plant to produce even more flowers.

### PLANT PROPERTIES ★★★★

**Shape and Size**

The quality of the plant allows this cultivar to produce so many flowers. It grows with enthusiasm and will be well branched, reaching up to 1.2m (4ft) tall and 75cm (2ft 6in) wide.

**Position**

Suited to any garden site, but for best results, avoid heavy shade.

**Hardiness**

Robust enough to withstand all but the most severe climates.

### FOLIAGE PROPERTIES

**Colour** ★★★

The attractive young foliage develops into large, dark green leaves. They provide the plant with a moderately full covering. In an ideal world there would be a few more.

**Health Check**

Only a moderate resistance to common problems. It will require protection from blackspot, and on occasion may suffer from downy mildew.

**Garden Uses**

Ideal for rose gardens or in a display of its own.

### OVERALL ASSESSMENT ★★★★

✔ A flower that will provide joy and happiness every year.

✖ The foliage is the weak point and it is not impervious to disease.

# Perception

## Bush Rose (Hybrid Tea)

### FLOWER PROPERTIES ★★★★★

**Colour**

Two contrasting colours make an appealing flower. The bulk of the petal is a golden cream; around the upper edge it is rose pink, which looks as if it has been sprayed on to the petal. The combination is very effective, and one of the wonders is how it can produce so many identical flowers when every one looks as if it was hand painted.

**Size and Shape**

Long, conical buds. Petals unfurl slowly, allowing us to enjoy the elegant pointed bud. As the flower approaches middle age the outer petals form a perfect circle while the inner petals still hold their high-centred point. When it reaches its fullest extent you can expect a flower of at least 13cm (5in) in diameter. It retains form and shape, yet has only 35 petals. Excellent in wet conditions.

**Scent**

Enjoy exploring the powerful scent, which is sweet, with a combination of rose and lemon.

**Production**

As is typical of pure hybrid tea roses, the flowers will often be borne as single blooms. They are on long, straight stems, just perfect for cutting. Produces plenty of flowers and repeats quickly and continuously into the late season.

### PLANT PROPERTIES ★★★

**Shape and Size**

Lots of vigour, maybe too much. The plant will throw up strong canes and, depending on conditions, may grow to between 1.4 and 2.4m (4ft 6in–8ft) tall. It will never become exceedingly bushy, expect 75cm–1.1m (2ft 6in–3ft 6in) wide. It can be kept under control by hard winter pruning, then, after flowering, but don't just deadhead, give it a moderate summer pruning.

**Position**

Grows with enthusiasm in any site. In a shady position it may get taller, growing up to look for light.

**Hardiness**

It is tough, and if it gets damaged it usually has the vigour to grow again.

### FOLIAGE PROPERTIES ★★★

**Colour**

The leaves are in proportion with the plant – that is, large. They are some of the most leathery-looking leaves you will see. Tough, thick and strong, in a rich green colour. Plenty are produced to give the plant a good covering.

**Health Check**

The main adversary of this cultivar is blackspot. Some measure of protection will be required.

**Garden Uses**

Only in positions that can cope with the size of the plant.

### OVERALL ASSESSMENT ★★★★

✔ This is the easiest way to grow a vase full of perfect blooms, and they have a good perfume.

✖ You may need a ladder to pick the flowers in some areas. Not as healthy as many other roses.

# Poetry in Motion

## Bush Rose (Hybrid Tea)

### FLOWER PROPERTIES ★★★★★

**Colour**
Saffron yellow suffused with pink as the flower ages. The colour is cheerful, and the injection of pink as the flower ages is not overpowering – only a light dusting to accompany the last few days of the flower.

**Size and Shape**
Large flowers spring out of long buds. This is a rose with poise and elegance. In the early stages the petals are draped around the tight, high-centred flower in distinct sculptured curves. As the flower develops, the length of the petals becomes evident. Retaining its attractive shape the flower will be over 10cm (4in) across, containing up to 35 petals.

**Scent**
Pleasant perfume with hints of citrus and honey.

**Production**
The large flowers are held singly or in clusters of no more than five buds. Repeat blooms quickly, so there are plenty of flowers to enjoy. Wonderful for cutting or in the garden.

### PLANT PROPERTIES ★★★★

**Shape and Size**
As with all good roses, it produces an even plant. Growth is vigorous, but not excessive. It will be between 1.1 and 1.4m (3ft 6in–4ft 6in) tall and around 1m (3ft) wide.

**Position**
Thrives in all but the shadiest positions.

**Hardiness**
Successful in all but the coldest regions.

### FOLIAGE PROPERTIES ★★★

**Colour**
Big leaves that look as if they have just returned from the beauty parlour, their gloss is so bright. They are mid-green, having grown though a youthful period of plum red. More than enough to cover the plant, creating a striking sight before the flowers arrive.

**Health Check**
Nothing is perfect, and this is no exception. Powdery mildew is its Achilles' heel.

**Garden Uses**
A valuable addition in any rose garden or bed or mixed border.

### OVERALL ASSESSMENT ★★★★

✔ A prolific producer of enchanting flowers.

✖ We may have to put up with a bit of powdery mildew.

# Pride of England

## Bush Rose (Hybrid Tea)

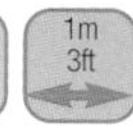

### FLOWER PROPERTIES ★★★

**Colour**

Deep blood red. The outer petals are almost black. The colour lasts well in all but the hottest sunshine. In very hot areas plant where there is some relief from intense sunlight.

**Size and Shape**

Classic in every detail – the petals intertwine in concentric circles creating the high centre of the flower. As it opens, the petals continue to unfurl, their size increasing but retaining the flower shape. Eventually all 35 petals will be on display. The bloom reaches 10cm (4in) across, and we will have had days of pleasure watching its progress.

**Scent**

The perfume is light and distinctive with undertones of spice.

**Production**

Perfect buds are produced on perfect long stems. An abundance of blooms continues throughout the season. Unlikely to produce clusters with more than three buds, but there are still plenty of flowers to make a dramatic impact.

### PLANT PROPERTIES ★★★

**Shape and Size**

A strong plant that produces a multitude of basal growths that ensure the plant will be wide and bushy. It will grow to an even height – expect 1.2–1.5m (4–5ft) tall and about 1m (3ft) wide.

**Position**

Anywhere except very strong sunlight in hottest areas.

**Hardiness**

Moderate; not one to try in the colder regions.

### FOLIAGE PROPERTIES ★★★★★

**Colour**

The leaf is unusual: mid-green underscored with a faint purple hue and with a matt finish. There will always be plenty of leaf to give good coverage over the plant.

**Health Check**

For a dark red rose its health is good. It suffers from blackspot only in adverse conditions.

**Garden Uses**

It will add stature to a rose garden or be a focal point in a mixed border.

### OVERALL ASSESSMENT ★★★★

✔ A reliable deep red rose. Good for cut flowers in the house.

✖ It would benefit from more perfume and a brighter colour.

# *Remember Me*

## Bush Rose (Hybrid Tea)

zone
7–8

FLOWER PROPERTIES ★★★★

**Colour**

An intriguing shade that explores the realms of copper and bronze. It is wonderful and unique but discolours badly in extremely hot sun.

**Size and Shape**

The shape is straight from the classic high-centred school. Faultlessly it opens its 35 petals, maintaining the structured form. When fully developed it will be over 9cm (3.5in) wide.

**Scent**

This rose is not grown for perfume; the colour is novel enough to forgive the absence of fragrance.

**Production**

Buds are produced in a combination of single blooms and clusters of up to five. They are numerous on the plant and, while the bush is never completely covered, the unexpected and rare colour will still amaze passers-by.

PLANT PROPERTIES ★★★★

**Shape and Size**

For one of the novelty colours the plant is excellent, growing with strong branches from the base to make an even bush of 1.1m (3ft 6in) tall and 75cm (2ft 6in) wide.

**Position**

Any position will grow a good plant. A little shade from the most intense sun is helpful.

**Hardiness**

Not ideal in the coldest regions.

FOLIAGE PROPERTIES ★★★★★

**Colour**

Light green and very shiny. The production of leaves is prolific, making the plant look full of vigour even on the lower parts of the bush.

**Health Check**

A report might say 'good effort, could try harder'. There can be blackspot attacks if the plant is under stress.

**Garden Uses**

Rose beds and borders or somewhere for an unusual colour.

OVERALL ASSESSMENT ★★★

✔ The colour in the garden or as a cut flower.

✖ You will have to keep on top of disease control to get the very best results.

# Renaissance

## Bush Rose (Hybrid Tea)

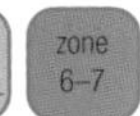


### FLOWER PROPERTIES ★★★★★

**Colour**

Shades that graduate from white to blush pink. The outer petals possess the paler tones, and the centre of the flower the pearl and blush shades. Petals resist damage from all but the heaviest rain.

**Size and Shape**

As the buds begin to open, they form the most perfect of flower shapes. Looking so delicate, a flower could easily be mistaken for the finest porcelain with its high centre and perfect circles of petals. When fully open the flower is large at 9cm (3.5in) across, but has only 25 petals to create this immaculate shape.

**Scent**

Powerful and pleasurable, with strong aromas of rose, citronella and honey.

**Production**

Flowers are either single or in clusters of no more than three buds. It is fortunate that each flower lasts well, otherwise the flowering density would be too low. Repeats well in the late season.

### PLANT PROPERTIES ★★★

**Shape and Size**

Makes a bush that has branches spreading out wide. It will not get very tall, no more than 1m (3ft), often less, with a width of 60cm (2ft).

**Position**

It is happiest in sun, but will perform adequately in semi-shade.

**Hardiness**

In contrast to the delicate appearance of the flower, the plant is hardy and worth a try in all regions.

### FOLIAGE PROPERTIES ★★★★★

**Colour**

The leaves are big, a little too large for the size of the plant. They form more easily on the upper half of the plant, on occasions leaving the bottom section a little bare. Dark green with a matt finish, they contrast perfectly with the flowers.

**Health Check**

Lacking in ideal behaviour. Powdery mildew is likely in the second half of the season. Blackspot will take advantage if the plant is stressed.

**Garden Uses**

Where the perfume will be appreciated.

### OVERALL ASSESSMENT ★★★★

✔ A flower that epitomizes all the virtues of the rose.

✖ A plant that cannot resist all the vices of a rose.

# *Royal William*

## Bush Rose (Hybid Tea)

zone
7–8

**FLOWER PROPERTIES** ★★★★

**Colour**

While the flower is young it is a rich, deep crimson. It behaves impeccably, with no sign of scorching in the sun and very little damage from rain. As the bloom reaches its final few days the colour fades, adopting a less attractive, bluish-red tinge. Best to deadhead at this stage.

**Size and Shape**

Flowers are large enough to satisfy all but the unreasonably demanding. With a shape that is a little on the rounded side, there are over 45 petals in the flower. It opens to an impressive 11cm (4.5in) across.

**Scent**

Rewarding without excelling. The flower colour leads us to anticipate a stronger perfume.

**Production**

A rose with larger-than-average flowers often lets itself down by not producing enough. This is an exception. The flowers are sometimes single or sometimes in clusters of no more than five. Two really good flushes of flower are produced in the season, each with plenty of flowers to make a memorable splash of colour.

**PLANT PROPERTIES** ★★★

**Shape and Size**

The canes that are produced by this rise ooze with strength and vitality. A free-growing plant that branches out, creating a substantial bush. Expect to see it grow to anything between 1.2 and 1.8m (4–6ft) tall, with a width of 75cm–1.1m (2ft 6in–3ft 6in).

**Position**

It will grow just about anywhere in the garden. Avoid areas of shade, which encourage it to grow taller in search of additional light.

**Hardiness**

Although it is very vigorous, it does not enjoy the coldest areas.

**FOLIAGE PROPERTIES** ★★★★★

**Colour**

The dark green leaves are abundant, large and finished with a dazzling gloss. There is plenty of leaf to give good coverage, which makes it an imposing spectacle.

**Health Check**

Resistant to assault from most diseases for most of the time. Blackspot may break down its defences in the second half of the season.

**Garden Uses**

Rose beds and gardens and anywhere that height is required.

**OVERALL ASSESSMENT** ★★★★

✔ A fine colour on a plant that is well behaved in most situations.

✖ The colour that the flower fades to spoils the look. It can be excessively tall.

# Savoy Hotel

## Bush Rose (Hybrid Tea )

1.1m
3.5ft

### FLOWER PROPERTIES ★★★★★

**Colour**

Light pink: a pure colour unadulterated by any foreign pigments. The only exception is on the outer petals, which retain a green tone that is soon hidden as the flower opens. The flowers keep their true colour, resisting any effort the sun makes to fade them, and are impervious to all but the heaviest rain.

**Size and Shape**

Round plump buds that are full of promise. Intricate and numerous rows of petals are arranged in wonderful symmetry, producing a flower with a perfectly formed centre. There are so many petals that the flower keeps its shape for days on end, eventually opening to 9cm (3.5in) across with 50 petals.

**Scent**

Not a strong perfume but a light rose and spice aroma.

**Production**

Flowers produced either as single blooms or in small clusters of no more than five, and the plant teems with blooms. It makes a great attempt to fully cover itself with blooms giving weeks of gardening pleasure. Provided the first flush is deadheaded and the plant is fed, there will be an equally fine second blooming.

### PLANT PROPERTIES ★★★

**Shape and Size**

A variety that produces an agreeably shaped bush, well rounded and dense, with many branches. Growing to 1.1m (3ft 6in) tall and 75cm (2ft 6in) wide, it is a useful garden plant.

**Position**

Good results in any position except heavy shade.

**Hardiness**

A tough and vigorous performer worth trying even in cold regions.

### FOLIAGE PROPERTIES ★★★★★

**Colour**

There is a lot of foliage on the plants and the leaves are an average size. Starting out as a ruby red colour, they grow to be mid-green with a matt finish.

**Health Check**

High resistance to most ailments, but blackspot may gain a foothold under stress.

**Garden Uses**

Will add colour to any rose bed or border.

### OVERALL ASSESSMENT ★★★★

✔ The consistent size and quality of the flowers.

✖ The colour is inoffensive but not inspiring. A good perfume would help.

# *Silver Anniversary*
## Bush Rose (Hybrid Tea)

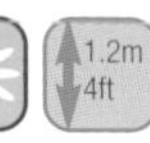

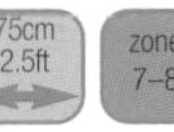


FLOWER PROPERTIES ★★★★

**Colour**
White. Uncomplicated simplicity with no subtle shades and variations.

**Size and Shape**
Large buds open to high-centred, elegant blooms. With 35 petals and at up to 8cm (3in) across, the flowers look good for an extended period.

**Scent**
A light spicey scent.

**Production**
For a hybrid tea this rose gives one of the most intense early displays. A large quantity of flowers cover the plant with abandon. With a solid performance in the late season there is little to complain about.

PLANT PROPERTIES

**Shape and Size** ★★★★
A robust plant, this creates an imposing, strong bush, with a tidy, rounded shape. There are plenty of stems making the plant look substantial. It grows to around 1.2m (4ft) tall and more than 75cm (2ft) across.

**Position**
It likes sunlight, so avoid shady positions.

**Hardiness**
Survives well in most regions but avoid the coldest.

FOLIAGE PROPERTIES ★★★★

**Colour**
The plant is covered with big, dark green, glossy leaves. There are plenty of them, giving a lovely contrast to the white flowers.

**Health Check**
Overall, a fine performer. Disease will not have any major or detrimental effect unless the plant is under stress.

**Garden Uses**
Formal rose gardens, beds and borders.

OVERALL ASSESSMENT ★★★★

✔ The total ease and reliability of the plant and flower.

✖ It lacks the 'wow' factor that stops us in our tracks.

# The McCartney Rose

## Bush Rose (Hybrid Tea)

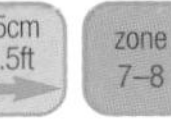

zone 7–8

FLOWER PROPERTIES ★★★

**Colour**

A mid- to deep pink: it is not a complex colour, and one of its attractions is its purity. This is not the best flower to withstand rain damage.

**Size and Shape**

The flowers are strikingly large, with the classic high-pointed centre of the hybrid tea. The 40 petals are put to great effect as the flower opens to 10cm (4in) across.

**Scent**

The real reason to grow this variety, it is strong, sweet and beautiful.

**Production**

Enough flowers to give a lot of pleasure, but production is on the shy side compared with many other modern roses. Late-season flowering is quite good.

PLANT PROPERTIES ★★★★

**Shape and Size**

Grows with enthusiasm to 1.2m (4ft) tall and 75cm (2ft 6in) across, forming a bush that is full of promise. There is adequate growth to make a good foundation to display the flowers.

**Position**

Not one of the best for a shady site.

**Hardiness**

Survives well in most regions but is not very hardy in the coldest.

FOLIAGE PROPERTIES ★★★

**Colour**

There are a lot of dark green leaves with a slight darker tint from the reddish spectrum.

**Health Check**

If conditions are against it there may be an attack of powdery mildew which may require chemical treatment.

**Garden Uses**

Best in rose beds or borders.

OVERALL ASSESSMENT ★★★

✔ The perfume will give unalloyed pleasure.

✖ The health record gives cause for concern. It would be nice to have a few more flowers.

# Warm Wishes

## Bush Rose (Hybrid Tea)

   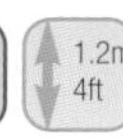

### FLOWER PROPERTIES ★★★★★

**Colour**

A confection of sweet pinks, salmons and a dash of yellow. A delightful flower, resilient in sun and rain.

**Size and Shape**

This is how a rose should be: it is blessed with the most pure and uncomplicated flower shape. The flowers may have only 35 petals, but these are used with devastating effect to create and keep that perfect rose shape. Up to 10cm (4in) across.

**Scent**

Combination of sweet rose and spice.

**Production**

The flowers come in small clusters, which produce a sequence of well-sized, perfect blooms. The repeat flowering is good, resulting in a plant that exceeds expectations by producing so many flowers.

### PLANT PROPERTIES ★★★★

**Shape and Size**

There is a strength and dominance to the plant. It says: 'Look at me, I'm wonderful.' Bushy, dense and even in its growth, it may reach 1.2m (4ft) tall and 75cm (2ft 6in) across.

**Position**

It will excel in all but the shadiest sites.

**Hardiness**

Slightly tender; it is advisable to protect it in cold climates.

### FOLIAGE PROPERTIES ★★★★★

**Colour**

The leaf is on the dark side but no less attractive for that. There will be a good covering, even low down on the plant. A strong leaf that is in proportion and harmony with the showy plant.

**Health Check**

With a good health record there is little trouble if the plant is not under stress.

**Garden Uses**

Perfect for rose beds, borders and gardens.

### OVERALL ASSESSMENT ★★★★

✔ A fine performer that will please the most demanding gardener.

✖ A little vulnerable in cold conditions.

# shrub
# roses

# *Armada*

## Shrub Rose

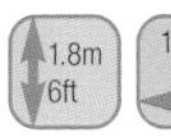

### FLOWER PROPERTIES ★★★★

**Colour**

Very pink. Not a colour to include in an area of restful, pastel shades. This is a pure, strong sugary pink that can be seen from a distance. The colour is stable in all weather conditions. The petals are firm and robust, and are able to resist wind and rain damage.

**Size and Shape**

The buds are rounded and small, around 4cm (1.5in) wide. One of the wonders of nature is how such large petals can come from such a small bud. There are only 10 petals, opening flat and showing the yellow of the stamens, which contrast brilliantly with the pink flowers.

**Scent**

Light, with a hint of musk combined with the rose scent.

**Production**

This is where we get our enjoyment. Clusters of up to 35 buds will open over a period that extends into weeks, not days. Excellent at repeat blooms in the late season if you deadhead the early blooms. In full flower a canopy of bloom completely covers the top of the plant.

### PLANT PROPERTIES ★★★★

**Shape and Size**

A really robust grower. The branches from the base will be thick and strong. It takes until the second or third season before it becomes a dense bush, and at this stage you will begin to see its true beauty. It will grow to 1.2–1.8m (4–6ft) tall and to 1–1.2m (3–4 ft) wide.

**Position**

As with all roses, it will perform best in a good position, but this is one to try in the more challenging sites. It is one of the toughest so expect good results in time.

**Hardiness**

Give winter protection in very cold areas.

### FOLIAGE PROPERTIES ★★★★

**Colour**

May be accused of having 'plain' foliage: light emerald green, shiny and attractive.

**Health Check**

Renowned for good health so ideal for beginners.

**Garden Uses**

Makes a great colourful hedge and gives colour in a mixed border.

### OVERALL ASSESSMENT ★★★★

✔ The health and strength of the plant, quantity of flower.

✖ The colour is a bit harsh in some circumstances.

# *Ballerina*
## Bush Rose (Shrub)

### FLOWER PROPERTIES ★★★

**Colour**

Soft, light pink around the outer petals pales to a white centre – a combination reminiscent of apple blossom. As the flowers age they will adopt a stronger pink shade. Flowers are unaffected by wind or rain, but in very strong sunshine they lose some of their beauty towards the end of their lives.

**Size and Shape**

Individual flowers are tiny and struggle to reach 2.5cm (1in) across. Opening from tiny, light green buds, they will be fully open, fresh and delightfully pretty in no time at all. There are just five petals surrounding the yellow stamens in the centre of the flower.

**Scent**

Not a cultivar that is selected for nasal appeal, as there is virtually no scent.

**Production**

Initial blooming commences a little late in the season, as many other roses are more than half-way through their first flush. However, it is worth waiting for. The clusters of flower buds are massive, creating flowerheads of well over 50 blooms, all opening in a sequence to produce a mass of delicate colour for weeks and weeks. The effect is more like a hydrangea than a rose.

### PLANT PROPERTIES ★★★★

**Shape and Size**

This is an easy plant to grow. It will naturally produce many basal shoots, giving a lovely bushy foundation to hold the striking flower heads. Expect a minimum height of 1.2m (4ft) and at least 1m (3ft) wide.

**Position**

This cultivar is strong and will grow in any fertile soil, but select a light position with some direct sunlight. If it is too shady, flowering will be late. Avoid very windy positions.

**Hardiness**

There is very little that nature can provide to upset this one.

### FOLIAGE PROPERTIES ★★★★

**Colour**

Leaves are light green, appearing in groups of 5, 7, 9 and on odd occasions 11. They are relatively long and narrow, but in sufficient quantity to make the plant well furnished.

**Health Check**

Has no terrible vices. There may be attacks of powdery mildew in the second half of the season.

**Garden Uses**

As an individual plant or wonderful in a mixed border.

### OVERALL ASSESSMENT ★★★

- ✔ The gift to share so many flowers with us is awesome.
- ✖ A little late to begin flowering. In hot weather the old flowers are unattractive until deadheaded.

# *Bonica*

## Bush Rose (Shrub)

### FLOWER PROPERTIES ★★★

**Colour**

Bright and cheerful, this is a simple rose pink. The colour is stable throughout the life of the flower. There are small variations of colour within the petal: it has a slightly lighter reverse, while the centre of the flower is a little deeper.

**Size and Shape**

Round buds open quickly to reveal an uncomplicated bloom with 15 petals. Wide and flat, about 6cm (2.5in) across, the flower is as simple in form as it is in colour.

**Scent**

You will appreciate any perfume only if your nose is more sensitive than mine.

**Production**

The plant will be festooned with flowers. It has a long flowering period and the initial burst of flowers will cover the plant and continue to do so for several weeks. Spectacular.

### PLANT PROPERTIES ★★★★★

**Shape and Size**

This plant forms a dense dome, rounded and even, producing a myriad of thin stems that will hold flowers all over its domed shape, blooming from just above ground to the top of the plant. Size varies according to conditions and pruning; expect it to be in the range of 1–1.4m (1–4ft 6in) tall and 75cm–1.1m (2ft 6in–3ft 6in) wide.

**Position**

Grows in fairly shady spots as well as sunny positions.

**Hardiness**

As with many pink roses, it is very hardy. Worth trying in all locations.

### FOLIAGE PROPERTIES ★★★

**Colour**

Leaves are mid- to light green, on the small side, but numerous. It is a pity that such a fine culitvar does not have more striking foliage.

**Health Check**

In most conditions health is good. Powdery mildew can be a problem in hot, dry periods. Plant in a position with good air circulation.

**Garden Uses**

In borders, beds or hedges where a splash of colour is required.

### OVERALL ASSESSMENT ★★★

✔ Easy to grow and ridiculously productive.

✖ The colour is a bit boring, unless you like plain pink.

# *Roxanthina Canary Bird*

## Bush Rose (Shrub)

3.6in 12ft
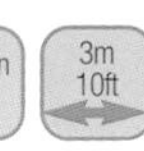

### FLOWER PROPERTIES ★★★

**Colour**

Here we have another simple, uncomplicated colour. No combination of shades, just an intense, bright yellow that remains the same throughout the life of the flower.

**Size and Shape**

With regard to flower size, the word small comes to mind. To continue the theme, we get small buds, small flowers – only five petals – opening to no more than 2.5cm (1in) across.

**Scent**

Sorry, nothing to enjoy in this department.

**Production**

It may be the first rose to bloom in the season but it does not repeat later. The flowers are delicately held along the length of the branches and are produced on tiny stalks on the old wood. Where the plant makes new stems, these will flower in future seasons but not in their first season.

### PLANT PROPERTIES ★★★★

**Shape and Size**

When it comes to size we have a different theme: big. The canes from the base may shoot up to between 2.4–3in (8–10ft). Mature dimensions can be up to 3.6m (12ft) tall and 3m (10ft) wide. The shape is divine: the long branches grow up and then arch gracefully downwards.

**Position**

With this amount of vigour any position is fine.

**Hardiness**

Tough in nearly all regions. Because it is tall it may suffer in windy sites.

### FOLIAGE PROPERTIES

**Colour** ★★★★★

The leaves are light green and are closely spaced along the stem. They have an unusual feathery appearance and the first impression is that they are fern-like. Good to use in flower arrangements – one of the few roses that has such a pretty leaf.

**Health Check**

Here we have a variety that is pretty well indestructible. Good resistance to plant ailments makes it easy to care for.

**Garden Uses**

Plant it only if you have a big space, at the back of a mixed border or as a specimen plant.

### OVERALL ASSESSMENT ★★★★

✔ Early flowering and pretty foliage.

✖ Short flowering period.

# Constance Spry

## Shrub Rose (Shrub)

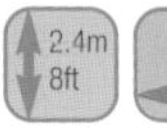

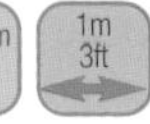

### FLOWER PROPERTIES ★★★★★

**Colour**

Light pink in all its stages, be it a young bud or fading flower. The colour is restful and tones down stronger colours in mixed plantings.

**Size and Shape**

Round buds open to supply blooms packed with petals. Curling and reflexing in orderly beauty, the 80 petals provide a wide flower to 8cm (3in) across. Good in all weather except heavy rain.

**Scent**

This is a flower that looks as if it should have perfume, and it does – a wonderful strong rose scent.

**Production**

The early flowering is a delight. Clusters of flowers adorn the bush, spaced at intervals that create a good cover. Enjoy the early flush for there will be little later in the season.

### PLANT PROPERTIES ★★★

**Shape and Size**

Growing to a tall bush that will be up to 2.4m (8ft) tall and 1m (3ft) wide. It is too tall and narrow for many uses and is susceptible to wind damage. The canes are long and whippy and in some areas may need support.

**Position**

Plant only in areas with good levels of light.

**Hardiness**

Survives well in most regions.

### FOLIAGE PROPERTIES ★★★★★

**Colour**

The leaf is mid- green without the polish we see on so many modern roses. There is a good quantity of leaf overall, apart from the lowest part of the plant.

**Health Check**

Usually holds its own against disease until late in the season.

**Garden Uses**

Best in mixed borders or shrub borders.

### OVERALL ASSESSMENT ★★★★

✔ The flower is a delight of delicacy and form.

✖ The habit of getting too tall and poor, late-season flowering.

# Cornelia

## Shrub Rose (Shrub)

### FLOWER PROPERTIES ★★★

**Colour**

Pink with undertones of peach. This is one of the roses that always exceeds my expectations. It is a simple blend of pinks , yet every year when it blooms my reaction is the same – I'd forgotten how beautiful it is.

**Size and Shape**

Little plump, round buds open to neat flowers containing 30 petals. Around 6cm (2.5in) across, they combine a gentleness with elegant charm.

**Scent**

An enjoyable perfume; a sweet musk is the usual conclusion.

**Production**

The early flush of flowers is the best, although in a good season late flowers can be prolific. The flowers are clustered, forming a pretty canopy of bloom over the plant.

### PLANT PROPERTIES

**Shape and Size** ★★★

Grows into a rounded shrub, with a multitude of branches making a dense bush. It is good at producing an even and attractive plant. Mature dimensions vary according to conditions and pruning but expect a minimum height of 1.2m (4ft), although it can get to 1.8m (6ft) tall. The width will be between 1.1-1.4m (3ft 6in–4ft 6in).

**Position**

Best to plant in a favourable position; it certainly needs good light.

**Hardiness**

This rose will struggle in colder regions.

### FOLIAGE PROPERTIES

**Colour** ★★★

Light green colour with a nice amount of gloss. The leaves are a good size but can be a little sparse on the plant.

**Health Check**

Powdery mildew is the main problem with this rose. Grow in sites and conditions to limit the damage that can be caused by powdery mildew.

**Garden Uses**

Best in mixed borders or shrub rose gardens.

### OVERALL ASSESSMENT ★★★★

✔ Combination of charm, scent and initial flowering.

✖ Foliage is not the best and repeat blooms can be poor in some seasons.

# Flower Carpet (Floral Carpet)

## Ground Cover Rose (Shrub)

FLOWER PROPERTIES ★★★

**Colour**

This rose is unfortunate in having a colour that I dislike, so I may not be complimentary about it. It is a deep pink, which always looks as if it is fighting to stay pink, with bluish-purple hues trying to distort the colour. To be fair, other people like the colour. For me, it is too harsh.

**Size and Shape**

The flowers are small, which is fine for this cultivar. They open from rounded buds and have about 25 petals. The petals retain a pretty concave shape as the flower opens to about 4cm (1.5in) in diameter. It has good tolerance of wet weather.

**Scent**

No joy in this area – there is no appreciable aroma.

**Production**

One of the more prolific flower producers. Flowers are produced along the stems in clusters, which are close to each other and become a sea of bloom. Capable of repeat blooming through the season, there are enough flowers to create a strong impact.

PLANT PROPERTIES ★★★★★

**Shape and Size**

The branches of this groundcover rose will start by growing upwards and outwards from the crown of the plant. As they lengthen, they begin to arch down, ending up as a mass of intermingled stems. Growing to a height of between 60cm and 1m (2–3ft) and a width of 1.2–1.8m (4–6ft) across, it will produce impenetrable groundcover.

**Position**

Good in any area, even heavily shaded.

**Hardiness**

It grows successfully in any area, so give it a go in cold, difficult locations.

FOLIAGE PROPERTIES ★★★★★

**Colour**

The foliage is the best feature of this cultivar. The leaves look as if they are coated in wax, are fairly dark green and radiate good health. Leaves are produced at close intervals along the stem, which helps it to create good groundcover.

**Health Check**

One of the roses to receive top marks in this area. If growing conditions are good there should be no ailments.

**Garden Uses**

Great for banks and slopes that you don't want grass on. Good in tubs and planters.

OVERALL ASSESSMENT ★★★★

✔ Outstanding health and freedom of flower.

✖ The colour leaves a little to be desired.

# *Gertrude Jekyll*

## Bush Rose (Shrub)

  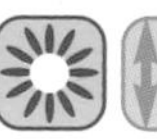 

1.2m
4ft

FLOWER PROPERTIES ★★★★★

**Colour**

A deep pink with intense depth. It is not a colour that varies much during the life of the flower. Only in hotter conditions does the flower begin to fade.

**Size and Shape**

The buds grow to be fat and plump before they open. It takes a while for the flower to become fully open, as there are so many rows of petals, all arranged to perfection. The flowers are big – it is not unusual to see them 10cm (4in) across – and with over 75 petals.

**Scent**

Don't get too close in case the scent overpowers you. Strong, sweet and intoxicatingly delightful.

**Production**

The flowers come in clusters, with the centre bloom flowering first. This will be the largest of the flowers, the remainder of the cluster being smaller. There are plenty of flowers but never a mass to cover the whole plant at once. Repeat blooming is reasonable in the late season.

PLANT PROPERTIES ★★★

**Shape and Size**

Established plants tend to be a bit leggy – there is a penchant for the lower half of the plant to be short of leaves and nothing more than a display of thorny old stems. According to the climate and pruning regime, the expected height is from 1.4 to 2.1m (4ft 6in–7ft) and a width of 1–1.2m (3–4ft). The plant will be more upright than bushy.

**Position**

Give it a site with plenty of sun and good ventilation.

**Hardiness**

Suitable in all but the coldest regions.

FOLIAGE PROPERTIES ★★★★

**Colour**

The colour is mid- green with a faint purple hue and matt finish. Leaves are plentiful on the upper half of the plant, sparse at lower levels. Although the leaves are large, they never look very robust, which may be because of the colour.

**Health Check**

Powdery mildew is the main concern. Unless preventative action is taken, the plant will suffer.

**Garden Uses**

An asset wherever perfume is required and the height can be accommodated.

OVERALL ASSESSMENT ★★★★

✔ The perfume and shape of the flower.

✖ Health and foliage could be better.

# Graham Thomas
## Shrub Rose (Shrub)

   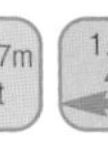

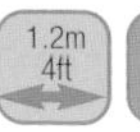

### FLOWER PROPERTIES ★★★★★

**Colour**
Primrose yellow with a hint of gold – a rare colour in a shrub of this type. It is a yellow with a lot of good qualities: it remains constant in all conditions, and the petals are strong, resisting any damage that the weather may try to inflict.

**Size and Shape**
Another rose that will produce big, round buds, full of promise. Buds opens slowly, providing a flower of ever more beauty as it develops. The petals retain a concave shape, as if protecting the centre of the flower and there are too many rows to count. With up to 75 petals crowded into a flower measuring up to 10cm (4in) across, we can gaze into this bloom with appreciative wonder.

**Scent**
A distinct and pleasing perfume but not overpowering.

**Production**
Coming in clusters of up to seven blooms, which open over an extended period, there is good continuity of flower. An able provider of bloom in the late season.

### PLANT PROPERTIES ★★★

**Shape and Size**
While the rose will grow well, it is likely to become too tall, making stems vulnerable to wind damage. Producing a good number of stems in a large plant gives it a dominant physical presence. Reaching between 1.5 and 2.7m (5–9ft) tall, but only 1–1.2m (3–4ft) wide, the size of this plant will vary according to local growing conditions.

**Position**
Must have an area with good light and some direct sunlight. Shade will make it too tall and weak.

**Hardiness**
Although the plant grows with vigour, it is not well suited to the coldest sites.

### FOLIAGE PROPERTIES ★★★

**Colour**
Rich dark green, large and well polished. Plenty of leaves gives the plant a good appearance, although they are less dense lower down where stems may become a bit bare and woody.

**Health Check**
This will not be one of the first to suffer from ill health. If there is an infection around it will fall victim to either blackspot or downy mildew, but it has good overall resistance.

**Garden Uses**
Ideal at the back of beds and borders where height is required.

### OVERALL ASSESSMENT ★★★★

- ✔ The best of the taller yellows, a strikingly beautiful flower.
- ✖ The growing habit can make it too tall, subject to wind damage, with too many flowers at the top and too few lower down.

# *Jacqueline du Pré*
## Bush Rose (Shrub)

### FLOWER PROPERTIES

**Colour**

Almost white, sometimes with a pink flush. One of the flower's unusual features are the red stamens in the centre. A resilient flower, it maintains its good looks in adverse conditions.

**Size and Shape**

Outstandingly pretty yet very simple. There are only 10 petals in the flower. It starts as a long conical bud, quickly opening to a flat flower where all the petals reflex and curve. Flowers average 8cm (3in) across.

**Scent**

For such a delicate flower the power of the perfume is a wonder. A combination of musk and lemon.

**Production**

Few roses are capable of producing more blooms in a year. They are borne in clusters, opening in a controlled sequence to maximize the life of every cluster. Flowering starts early, sometimes four weeks before other bush roses. The repeat is rapid, and three flushes in a season are to be expected.

### PLANT PROPERTIES ★★★★

**Shape and Size**

A wide and bushy specimen. Average dimensions will be 1.4m (4ft 6in) tall by 1.1m (3ft 6in) wide. It produces an impenetrable matted mass of stems, which work hard to support the mass of flowers.

**Position**

A hardy plant, it will accept any position, even places where there is shade.

**Hardiness**

Possessing a strong constitution, it is worth trying in both hospitable and hostile positions.

### FOLIAGE PROPERTIES

**Colour** ★★★

The leaf has a matt finish and a mid- to dark green shade. It is not one of the attractive leaves – more of a functional item than a beauty accessory.

**Health Check**

There is little disease where growing conditions are managed well. If there are any problems it will be blackspot in the second half of the season.

**Garden Uses**

It is so amenable and flexible that it will enhance any garden.

### OVERALL ASSESSMENT ★★★★

✔ Extremely long flowering; scent and flower beauty.

✖ Let down by the quality of the leaf and some blackspot.

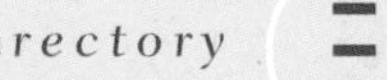

# Marjorie Fair

## Bush Rose (Shrub)

  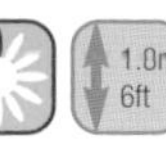 

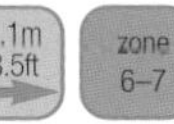

zone 6–7

### FLOWER PROPERTIES ★★★

**Colour**

The two distinct colours are cerise and white, divided into concentric circles. The central section of the flower is white, and the outer ring is cerise, making a bold effect. Flowers endure any amount of wet weather, but in high intensity sunlight they fade badly as they age. Deadheading keeps the appearance attractive.

**Size and Shape**

There will be hundreds of tiny, light green buds on this plant. Each will open into a bloom of no more than 2.5cm (1in) across. They have only five petals arranged wide open in a circle.

**Scent**

In spite of the quantity of flowers produced, the scent is negligible.

**Production**

Produced in vast clusters, tightly packed together, there is the potential to have a complete sea of bloom covering the plant. Repeat blooms well in the late season.

### PLANT PROPERTIES ★★★★

**Shape and Size**

A thicket of stems is produced from the base of the plant. It will be dense and impenetrable, growing to 1.2–1.8m (4–6ft) tall and 75cm–1.1m (2ft 6in–3ft 6in) wide.

**Position**

Anywhere in the garden. In hot areas avoid full sun.

**Hardiness**

Renowned for its hardiness and worth trying in any region.

### FOLIAGE PROPERTIES ★★★★★

**Colour**

The leaves are small and numerous. With a mid- to light green shade and matt appearance, they are not the most attractive. Best considered as being functional rather than beautiful. They fulfil the functional role with aplomb, clothing the plant in a dense and even green coat.

**Health Check**

As healthy as it is hardy. Impervious to most attacks, with the exception of powdery mildew in the late season.

**Garden Uses**

Hedges and mixed borders will exploit its strengths.

### OVERALL ASSESSMENT ★★★★

✖ Ease of culture and productivity.
The colour of the old flowers can deteriorate if you don't deadhead.

# Mme Isaac Pereire

## Shrub Rose (Shrub)

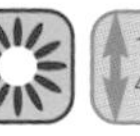

### FLOWER PROPERTIES ★★★★

**Colour**

There is richness in the deep crimson to purple colour. It is one of those roses that are tactile: you have to feel the petals as well as look at them. They feel soft, which is lovely, except it means that they are susceptible to rain damage, which may spoil the flower by making brown spots on the petals. Petals discolour as they age, taking on a bluish tinge.

**Size and Shape**

Large, cupped flowers up to 10cm (4in) across, with around 50 petals arranged in a neat, symmetrical, intricate pattern. Each is a work of art to be savoured and enjoyed.

**Scent**

Heady and intoxicating on a balmy day. Another cultivar that should be in the top ten.

**Production**

There are just enough flowers, but more would be nice. They are borne in small clusters spread around the plant, without covering it densely. A pleasing first flush is followed by an even sparser second flush.

### PLANT PROPERTIES ★★★

**Shape and size**

A bold, tall plant of significant stature, growing to at least 1.8m (6ft) high and 1.2m (4ft) wide. The plant produces plenty of stems, making a dense shrub.

**Position**

Requires reasonable light, so avoid medium to heavily shaded areas.

**Hardiness**

It is worth trying everywhere, for the scent alone. Protection is required in colder regions.

### FOLIAGE PROPERTIES ★★★

**Colour**

Mid- green foliage can have a slight grey undertone. The leaves are not the strongest aspect, less attractive many other cultivars.

**Health Check**

An acceptable level of health, but it needs watching. Both powdery mildew and blackspot can be problems and remedial action will be required to prevent heavy attacks.

**Garden Uses**

At the back of borders because it flowers mostly at the top and the shorter plants in front will not hide many blooms.

### OVERALL ASSESSMENT ★★★

- ✔ The flower will satisfy three senses: sight, touch and smell.
- ✖ Not healthy enough to survive without attention and work

# Nevada

## Shrub Rose (Shrub)

FLOWER PROPERTIES ★★

**Colour**

Fluctuating between cream and white, with the occasional flush of pink. The pink appears as the flowers are finishing. They begin cream and fade to a near white before petal fall.

**Size and Shape**

Measuring around 5cm (2in) across when fully open, they are pretty little flowers with five petals. A fine example of how something simple can be both beautiful and elegant.

**Scent**

A light but a perceptible offering that has hints of citrus.

**Production**

Only one decent flush of flower – one spectacular display, with nothing in the autumn. Buds are produced all over the plant, from almost ground level to the top – a sight to relish.

PLANT PROPERTIES ★★★★

**Shape and Size**

Imagine a plant that is up to 3m (10ft) tall and 2.4m (8ft) wide. It is large, the branches arch, tier after tier of them making a neat, rounded bush. The lowest branches just brush the ground, while the highest grow straight up the centre of the plant.

**Position**

If you have a big space, even in shade, it will fill it for you.

**Hardiness**

Worth trying in exposed or cold sites and excellent in favourable positions.

FOLIAGE PROPERTIES ★★★

**Colour**

Small leaves abound. They could be at closer intervals on the plant, which could look better furnished with leaf, but there are enough to cover most of the stems. Light in colour, matt in appearance, they do a workmanlike job without venturing into the realms of beauty.

**Health Check**

This is a strong rose. Few ailments attack this plant.

**Garden Uses**

Ideal as a specimen plant or for the back of borders. It must have space to thrive.

OVERALL ASSESSMENT ★★★

✔ That one flush of flower is enough to earn it a place in any garden.

✖ The size may be a drawback, as is the inability to produce a second flush of flower.

# *Rosa glauca (R.rubrifolia)*
## Shrub Rose (Shrub)

### FLOWER PROPERTIES ★★★★★

**Colour**
The most insignificant flower in this book. It is a species that earns its inclusion by a multitude of attributes other than its flower. The flower is light pink graduating to white. This rose also produces a veritable cascade of bright red hips in autumn.

**Size and Shape**
The flowers are small, less than 2.5cm (1in) across, with five petals. They are pretty in their own way but not really significant. The hips are rounded but not quite a perfect sphere. They will be about 1cm (½in) across.

**Scent**
The flowers are gone before you have chance to check it, and, if you do, there is very little there.

**Production**
The plant is festooned with flowers early in the season. It will not repeat, and the flowers last only a few days. The hips turn red in very late summer or early autumn. Like the flowers they will also cover the plant, but unlike the flowers, they remain visible and enjoyable for a long time. It is not unusual for hips to still be present at midwinter.

### PLANT PROPERTIES ★★★

**Shape and Size**
Big in all dimensions, it will produce a woody thicket all on its own. With arching branches to 2.7m (9ft) tall, and a width of up to 1.8m (6ft), this is a specimen that requires space.
It will not respond happily to attempts to confine it.

**Position**
Provides satisfaction wherever it is planted.

**Hardiness**
Worth trying in all regions.

### FOLIAGE PROPERTIES ★★★★★

**Colour**
Here we stumble across another reason for growing this species. The leaf is small for such a large plant, and the colour is unusual. It retains a purple tint throughout the season. During the first half in particular the foliage is very pretty – it is an asset in flower arrangements.

**Health Check**
Few health problems here. If the plant is afflicted with any ailment it has enough vigour to survive the attack.

**Garden Uses**
Where the foliage and hips can be enjoyed, as a specimen or at the back of a mixed border.

### OVERALL ASSESSMENT ★★★★

- ✔ The leaf and hips give this interest when other roses may not be at their best.
- ✖ It needs a lot of space. The flower is only fleeting.

# *Sally Holmes*

## Shrub Rose (Shrub)

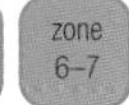


### FLOWER PROPERTIES ★★★★★

**Colour**

Cream and honey are the dominant colours. They blend together and have a tendency to fade to white as the flower ages. It is a pretty fade and not one that disfigures or detracts from the colour of the younger flowers.

**Size and Shape**

Big, wide, flat flowers with just five petals open, up to 10cm (4in) across.

**Scent**

Light, fresh and enjoyable perfume – not a lot from individual flowers, but adequate collectively.

**Production**

Big clusters of blooms with over 40 buds to a cluster. The plant will be covered in clusters, and when it is in full flower there is nothing but flower on show. Flowers open sequentially in the clusters giving an extended flowering period. Repeat flowers in the late season.

### PLANT PROPERTIES ★★★

**Shape and Size**

A substantial bush in all dimensions. The growth is sturdy, holding the heavy flowerheads proudly. It reaches between 1.4 and 2.4m (4ft 6in–8ft) tall, with a width of between 1 and 1.5m (3–5ft).

**Position**

It will grow in sunny or shady sites.

**Hardiness**

There is a strength and resilience to the plant, but it requires protection in the coldest regions.

### FOLIAGE PROPERTIES

**Colour** ★★★★★

The plant would look better if it was clothed with more leaves, which can become sparse on the lower branches of the plant. The leaves are attractive, although they would be a better foil for the flower if they were a darker shade of green.

**Health Check**

Strong resistance to disease, but powdery mildew can put in an appearance late in the season.

**Garden Uses**

Mixed borders, hedges or as a specimen plant.

### OVERALL ASSESSMENT ★★★★

✔ The outstandingly beautiful flower, which is also good as a cut flower.

✖ The foliage is mediocre, and the colour insipid to some people.

# Scabrosa

## Shrub Rose (Shrub)

    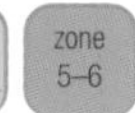


FLOWER PROPERTIES ★★★★★

**Colour**
Rich magenta with hints of purple. A colour that will make you stop and look, to appreciate its beauty fully. Yellow stamens in the centre of the flower create a bold contrast. In the late season there will be tomato-red hips for added colour.

**Size and Shape**
The flowers open into large, flat blooms, the five petals opening wide to make the flower over 8cm (3in) across. The hips are of equal stature, fleshy, plump and round. They will be at least 2.5cm (1in) in diameter.

**Scent**
The flower may not have many petals, but it has abundant perfume. Strong and sweet, it is a real rose fragrance.

**Production**
Flowers in clusters strategically placed over the bush make a prolific early flowering. Unusually for a variety with a showy display of hips, these will be followed by a reasonable late season flush. Hips will mature to tomato-red in very late summer and will be there to enjoy until well into winter.

PLANT PROPERTIES ★★★

**Shape and Size**
A mature bush will be big and wide. A matted confusion of branches make the bush rounded in shape, and up to 2.4m (8ft) tall by 1.5m (5ft) wide. Each branch is covered in very fine, sharp thorns, more like prickly hairs than normal thorns.

**Position**
A plant that is able to contend with any position you give it.

**Hardiness**
Try in cold zones as well as more temperate areas.

FOLIAGE PROPERTIES ★★★★★

**Colour**
The foliage is a distinctive, light green with a wrinkled appearance. It looks hard wearing and covers the plant with an impenetrable mass of leaf. As the leaves fall they turn yellow.

**Health Check**
Full marks for its ability to resist any attack.

**Garden Uses**
At the back of borders, as hedge or as a specimen plant.

OVERALL ASSESSMENT ★★★★

✔ Bullet-proof health and hardiness; great hips.

✖ A few more flowers that lasted longer would be a big improvement.

# The Fairy

## Bush Rose (Shrub)

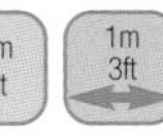

### FLOWER PROPERTIES ★★★★

**Colour**

A soft, warm rose pink, steadfast regardless of the weather – sun and rain make little impression.

**Size and Shape**

The small flowers are 4cm (1.5in) across with 35 petals. Flowers are rounded, with petals that crinkle and curl prettily into the centre.

**Scent**

Best described as absent.

**Production**

This rose has an amazing ability to flower. It becomes a mound of pink with flowers everywhere. A little late to start flowering, but worth every minute of the wait.

### PLANT PROPERTIES ★★★★

**Shape and Size**

An individual rose will grow to about 1m (3ft) tall, forming a rounded mound, as wide as it is tall. The branches grow up and then arch gracefully down, allowing it to flower from the ground upwards.

**Position**

A versatile plant, happy in sun or partial shade.

**Hardiness**

Give protection in the coldest areas for a good display.

### FOLIAGE PROPERTIES ★★★★

**Colour**

Another charming feature of this variety. The leaves are a fresh, light green with a deep polish. They are small and produced in a density that covers the plant completely.

**Health Check**

Nothing to worry about. An occasional attack of powdery mildew is about all you will see with this hardy rose.

**Garden Uses**

Borders, patio tubs and mixed plantings.

### OVERALL ASSESSMENT ★★★★

✔ It is unusual and very colourful and grows easily.

✖ It likes to grow wide and will get shabby if it isn't pruned.

# climbing roses

# *Albéric Barbier*

## Climbing Rose (Rambler)

### FLOWER PROPERTIES ★★★

**Colour**

The effect is overwhelmingly cream. Combinations of off-whites and light yellows produce a bright, light effect. There is very little colour fade, as the original flower is a combination of light shades. The only adverse reaction is to suffer from bruising and marking in wet conditions

**Size and Shape**

The flowers open from rounded buds to flat blooms. They are pretty as individual flowers, because the petals are crammed into dense circles of unfurling beauty. The fully open flower will be up to 8cm (3in) across, containing about 70 petals.

**Scent**

Not renowned for its perfume but possessing a light musky scent

**Production**

Produces flowers in abundant clusters early in the season. If most of the old flowerheads are removed there will be a few blooms later on.

### PLANT PROPERTIES ★★★

**Shape and Size**

A vigorous climbing plant. It can grow up to 7.5m (25ft) tall, covering a width of 4.5m (15ft). It produces long climbing canes that are easy to train against a structure because the canes are long and flexible, it is suitable to train in a position that requires a long low plant – such as a 1.2m (4ft) wall – as well as traditional tall spaces. Not a cultivar to grow in a small space. Unless you have an area in excess of 10 sq m (about 110 sq ft), it's best to miss this one.

**Position**

Requires a light position, with partial sunlight. Good soil is necessary for the best results

**Hardiness**

Will grow in most areas, but in cold climates place it where it will be protected from strong winter and spring winds.

### FOLIAGE PROPERTIES ★★★★

**Colour**

The leaves are dark in colour with a sheen that makes them an attractive feature. They are medium in size and will often be produced in groups of 7, 9 or even 11 leaves.

**Health Check**

A rose that will shake off most attacks, as long as it is fit and strong with good growing conditions

**Garden Uses**

Grow up or along any structure that is big enough to accommodate its vigorous nature. It may be grown into established trees.

### OVERALL ASSESSMENT ★★★

✔ Good health and ease of care. The flowers are beautiful individually and effective *en masse* on the plant.

✖ Not a good second flowering season, and the blooms may be damaged by wet weather.

# Bridge of Sighs
## Climbing Rose

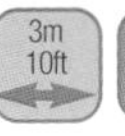

### FLOWER PROPERTIES ★★★★

**Colour**

Gold infused with peach tones is a rare colour in a climber. The colour remains stable as the petals age; a little more of the peach tones comes through in hotter conditions.

**Size and Shape**

Small buds open quickly into simple flowers with 10 petals. One of the unusual features of the flower is the way the petals are frequently pointed, giving a charming shape to the wide open flower. The blooms average 6cm (2.5in) in across.

**Scent**

Surprisingly strong for a small flower; sweet, with hints of honey and lemon.

**Production**

Flower production can be summed up in one word – prodigious. Clusters of flower start early in the season and repeat with astonishing rapidity.

### PLANT PROPERTIES ★★★★★

**Shape and Size**

A climber with long canes that are easy to train if you allow them to ripen before you bend them too much. It produces plenty of basal shoots to use to create a good framework. The lateral shoots that bear the flowers are not too long and are quick to grow. You will be able to train it to anything from 1.8 to 3.6m (6–12ft) tall and 1.8–3m (6–10ft) wide.

**Position**

It will be happy in an open position. Partial sunlight is also acceptable

**Hardiness**

Not suited to colder regions where it will be susceptible to winter frost damage.

### FOLIAGE PROPERTIES

**Colour** ★★★★

Initially leaves are deep red, which is an attractive stage. They turn dark green, with a non-gloss shine.

**Health Check**

When the plant is in full flower it requires copious amounts of water to maintain health. If allowed to become stressed it is vulnerable to blackspot.

**Garden Uses**

Wherever a climber is required, except in heavy shade or a north-facing site.

### OVERALL ASSESSMENT ★★★★★

✔ A great colour for a climber, with good scent.

✖ Not a lot, but requires plenty of food and water to get the best results.

# Compassion
## Climbing Rose

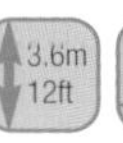

### FLOWER PROPERTIES ★★★★★

**Colour**

A combination of shades, including pink, salmon and peach tones, combine to produce a pretty confection of colour. Colour varies with daylight length and sunlight intensity, becoming more salmon coloured with longer warmer days.

**Size and Shape**

Large, plump and rounded buds open into young blooms with a pointed centre. As they progress to large, cupped flowers, the full array of colours blends together. Large flowers, 10cm (4in) across, have around 45 petals each.

**Scent**

Exquisite perfume, really strong from an individual flower. Massed on a plant, it is almost overpowering.

**Production**

A repeat-flowering climber, having two highly rewarding flushes of flower. Spectacular in full bloom and managing to flower from low down to the top of the plant.

### PLANT PROPERTIES ★★★★

**Shape and Size**

A climber with reasonable vigour, it can be trained easily. The stems are slightly stiff, so it important to train them in the period after they begin to ripen but before they become too stiff. It will grow to 3.6m (12ft) high and to 2.4m (8ft) across.

**Position**

Happy growing up any structure, but do not plant on a north-facing aspect.

**Hardiness**

Thrives in all conditions.

### FOLIAGE PROPERTIES ★★★

**Colour**

The leaves are large and dark green. There are plenty of them to create a good background to complement the flowers.

**Health Check**

In the late season it may suffer from a light dose of powdery mildew or blackspot. It is not overly susceptible to these ailments but maintaining good growing conditions reduces the chance of disease.

**Garden Uses**

Up any structure that requires a climbing plant.

### OVERALL ASSESSMENT ★★★★

✔ Has a better perfume than almost any other repeat-flowering climber.

✖ Needs to be cosseted and given good conditions to prevent foliage troubles.

# Della Balfour
## Climbing Rose

zone 7–8

### FLOWER PROPERTIES ★★★★

**Colour**

A colour of interest and beauty. A gentle meeting of oranges and yellows, the colours of fire, which combine in a restful, complementary way. As the flower ages, it becomes infused with pink.

**Size and Shape**

Large buds open to reveal long petals and at first the blooms use this length of petal to form elegant young flowers. These become round, cupped blooms of 30 petals. Each flower can be up to 10cm (4in) across when fully open.

**Scent**

Endowed with a subtle, spicy musk perfume.

**Production**

Flowers in groups of three or five. Smaller clusters than many climbers, but the extra size of the blooms helps to give good coverage. It repeats well in the later season.

### PLANT PROPERTIES ★★★

**Shape and Size**

A climber with moderate vigour, making it an option for confined spaces. The canes are sturdy and less pliable than average for a climber. It is ideal for training as a traditional fan shape. The mature height will be between 2.1 and 3.3m (7–11ft), spreading 1.8–2.7m (6–9ft) wide.

**Position**

Requires some direct sunlight. Avoid heavy shade, northwest, north or northeast aspects.

**Hardiness**

Will be happy in all but the coldest regions.

### FOLIAGE PROPERTIES ★★★

**Colour**

Starting off a rich red, the leaves progress to mid- green at maturity. They are large, robust leaves that offer a good foil to the flowers.

**Health Check**

Susceptible to blackspot when under stress, so keep well fed. Good culture will reduce the severity of any attacks of blackspot.

**Garden Uses**

On walls or fences or up a trellis.

### OVERALL ASSESSMENT ★★★★

✔ The colours are wonderful in a climber.

✖ Not the hardiest nor the easiest to train.

# Dublin Bay
## Climbing Rose

zone
7

FLOWER PROPERTIES ★★★

**Colour**
Deep red, deepest at the outer edge of the petals. Unlike many reds, the colour is stable as the flower ages, even in bright sunlight. It may suffer from some spotting in wet weather.

**Size and Shape**
The buds are conical, opening to reveal a flower that develops quickly into a large, open bloom of 10cm (4in) across. There are only 20 petals, but they last well and provide pleasure for days on end.

**Scent**
A disappointment: this red has virtually no perfume.

**Production**
In clusters of five or seven, blooms open in sequence to provide a good duration of flower. Repeating well, there will be plenty of flowers throughout the season.

PLANT PROPERTIES ★★★★

**Shape and Size**
Restrained and controllable growth by the standards of the average climbing rose. It generates a plethora of stems that provide good cover for the structure against which it is grown. An anticipated height of 2.4–3.6m (8–12ft) and 1.5–2.4m (5–8ft) wide.

**Position**
A tough customer, although not highly vigorous. It will grow in most positions, even shady sites.

**Hardiness**
No special treatment required. Worth trying in all regions.

FOLIAGE PROPERTIES ★★★★

**Colour**
The leaves are on the dark side, which is a pity, because a dark green leaf is not the best colour to show off a deep red flower. The leaves are large and plentiful, giving good coverage.

**Health Check**
Acceptable resistance to the ailments that nature throws into the garden, but not perfect. The main concern is blackspot and, in some seasons, a little powdery mildew. Best to avoid planting in areas that will exacerbate these problems.

**Garden Uses**
Over walls, fences and low structures, including pergolas and arches.

OVERALL ASSESSMENT ★★★

✔ That wonderful colour, which is repeated through the season.

✖ Weak on the health front.

# François Juranville
## Climbing Rose (Rambler)

  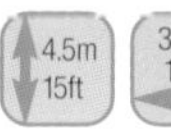

### FLOWER PROPERTIES ★★★★

**Colour**

There is an enduring warmth to the colour. A simple rose pink that pleases the eye and sparks a feeling of well-being. Unfortunately, the colour is not perfect: it will fade in intense sunlight. Even worse, heavy rain turns some petals to a soft, brown, decaying pulp.

**Size and Shape**

Bursting from plump, round buds, the flowers are full of charm and promise. As each bud opens, it keeps on delighting us with more and more petals, which curl and reflex prettily, with the smallest ones crowded into the centre of the bloom. The wide open flower measures to 10cm (4in) across.

**Scent**

The welcome sweetness of a traditional rose perfume wafts from the flowers.

**Production**

Flowers appear on short lateral stems along the main branches. They are plentiful, giving a good cover of bloom. The only downside is that there is not a strong showing after the first flush, just sporadic flowers.

### PLANT PROPERTIES ★★★★★

**Shape and Size**

A plant that always exhibits plenty of vigour. The climbing shoots can grow up to 3m (10ft) long and have good flexibility, making them a pleasure to train against a structure. Once the initial framework of the plant is established, it will fill in with strong lateral growths. Growing up to 4.5m (15ft) tall by 3.6m (12ft) wide it is able to create a stunning impact.

**Position**

Although it will be happy in most positions, reasonable light levels are needed for it to excel.

**Hardiness**

A hardy specimen, it does not enjoy the coldest regions without protection from winter winds.

### FOLIAGE PROPERTIES ★★★

**Colour**

Mid- green in colour with a well-polished surface. The colour of the leaf works very well, and there are plenty of leaves to provide a backdrop for the flowers.

**Health Check**

Considering the age of the cultivar it is remarkably good at repelling the ailments that can attack roses. Depending on conditions, there may be some powdery mildew or blackspot, but not heavy attacks.

**Garden Uses**

Grow as a climber on any structure in a light position. If you can find it as a weeping standard (tree rose), it makes a beautiful plant.

### OVERALL ASSESSMENT ★★★

✔ The combination of old-world charm and robust nature. Stunning when grown as a weeping standard.

✖ Failure to have a decent second flush of flowers.

# High Hopes
## Bush Rose (Climber)

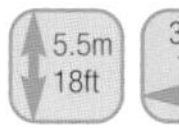

### FLOWER PROPERTIES ★★★★

**Colour**

The result is a pink flower, but the ingredients that make the colour are complex. A range of colours, from a creamy pink to a light salmon pink, blend together to make a pretty bloom. The petals are firm and resist damage from wind, sun and rain.

**Size and Shape**

Long petals provide a classic high-centred bloom as the bud begins to open. Opening into a bloom of 6cm (2.5in) across, 25 petals form a long-lasting, round circular flower.

**Scent**

An enjoyable and reasonably powerful perfume.

**Production**

Produces clusters of up to five blooms, which all last well, resulting in a long flowering period. A good second flush of flowers late in the season makes this a rewarding climber.

### PLANT PROPERTIES ★★★★

**Shape and size**

Producing long vigorous climbing stems, it grows into a large climbing plant between 3 and 5.5m (10–18ft) tall and 1.8–3.6m (6–12ft) wide, depending on conditions and pruning. The stems are not too thick, making them pliable and easy to train.

**Position**

A robust performer that will grow on any aspect.

**Hardiness**

Worth trying in all areas, although some protection may be required in the coldest regions.

### FOLIAGE PROPERTIES ★★★★

**Colour**

Starting red and turning to mid-green, the leaves are close together and large. Well furnished with foliage, making a good green background for the flowers.

**Health Check**

A cultivar with very good disease resistance. If it grows without any stress it will remain healthy.

**Garden Uses**

Great on walls, fences and large arches or pergolas.

### OVERALL ASSESSMENT ★★★★

✔ There are no obvious faults; it is competent in all respects.

✖ Competent in all respects, but a shame that it excels in none.

# Kiftsgate (Filipes Kiftsgate)
## Climbing Rose (Rambler)

zone 5

FLOWER PROPERTIES ★★★★★

**Colour**
White, with prominent yellow stamens in the centre of the flower.

**Size and Shape**
Tiny buds open to tiny flowers. They have five petals and measure no more than 2.5cm (1in) across. Flowers remain clean and bright until the petals fall, resisting rain damage with ease.

**Scent**
Individual flowers have a tiny amount of scent. A plant covered in them fills an area of the garden with a sweet combination of vanilla and banana.

**Production**
Flower clusters are large and impressive. There may be over 100 buds in a big cluster. The rose starts to flower later than most types, providing bloom when others are finishing their first flush of flower. The flowers open over a period of a few weeks. Unfortunately, there is no worthwhile late flowering.

★★★

PLANT PROPERTIES

**Shape and Size**
This is about the most vigorous climbing rose there is. It will grow up to 10.5m (35ft) tall and 7.5m (25ft) wide. It can be kept a bit smaller, but do not try to restrict it to a small area – it likes to fill big spaces. The long stems are very pliable and easy to train.

**Position**
Try covering a barn or fence. This rose can be grown into trees, including conifers, adding flowers where they are not expected.

**Hardiness**
If it won't grow, your conditions are very testing.

★★★★

FOLIAGE PROPERTIES

**Colour**
Light in colour, the leaves are in groups of anything from 5 to 13. The plant produces them at remarkably close intervals, making a dense blanket of foliage.

**Health Check**
The constitution is tough. Nothing appears to stop its advance. If disease attacks the plant it will continue to grow regardless.

**Garden Uses**
Suitable only where there is adequate space. Grow into trees and hedges for additional interest.

★★★★

OVERALL ASSESSMENT

✔ Easy to grow; will cover awkward and difficult areas with verve.

✖ Shorter flowering period than we would like. Needs a lot of space.

# Little Rambler
## Climbing Rose (Climber)

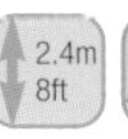

### FLOWER PROPERTIES ★★★

**Colour**

The buds are light pink when they are young and beginning to open. As the flower develops, it will pale to a soft pearl shade, and in the final stage the bloom will be white before petal fall.

**Size and Shape**

Rounded buds are small, but plump. They open to semi-double flowers, no more than 5cm (2in) across. The petals are tightly packed as they unfurl from the tight bud, and then the yellow centre of the flower smiles out from a flat, open flower.

**Scent**

Only a light perfume; a waft of rose scent can be found on a warm summers evening.

**Production**

Unlike the ramblers of old, this is a repeat-flowering cultivar. It will provide two good main flushes of flower. The flowers are born in clusters, so although the individual flowers are small the dense clusters will ensure that there is a big splash of colour for a long time.

### PLANT PROPERTIES ★★★★★

**Shape and size**

As the name suggests, it is little for a rambler, growing to between 1.8 and 2.4m (6-8ft) tall and to 2.1m (7ft) wide. It has all the attributes of a rambler: long, slender stems that are easy to train, plenty of vigour and a robust constitution, but all this is within a small and manageable framework.

**Position**

Grow in any location, except heavy shade.

**Hardiness**

This is a tough rose, much tougher than the slender stems would have you imagine.

### FOLIAGE PROPERTIES

**Colour** ★★★

The leaves are small, in perfect proportion with the plant, and are light to mid-green with a well-polished, attractive appearance. There are just enough of them to make a good background to the flowers.

**Health Check**

As with many vigorous plants, the overall health of this variety is good when growing well. You will have to protect a plant in less than ideal conditions and some stress from both powdery and downy mildew.

**Garden Uses**

A rewarding rose to grow on fences, walls or small pergolas.

### OVERALL ASSESSMENT ★★★★

✔ All the charm and beauty of an old rambler in a compact and manageable plant.

✖ Although there are lots of flowers, the colour is a little weak, with some further fade.

# Mermaid
## Climbing Rose (Climber)

zone 8

### FLOWER PROPERTIES ★★★★

**Colour**
Light primrose yellow. There are occasions when it seems a little paler, but it is always pretty. In most conditions there is a perceptible or detrimental change to the colour as the flower ages.

**Size and Shape**
With just five petals and a flower frequently over 8cm (3in) in diameter, it is easy to imagine that the individual petals are large. When it is fully open, the flower is a real beauty, exhibiting deep yellow stamens.

**Scent**
While there is not a lot of perfume, there is a musky aroma from a plant covered in bloom.

**Production**
With clusters spread evenly all over the plant there is no shortage of bloom, and it flowers for a long period. Because individual blooms are so large it is striking even when there are not many flowers on the plant.

### PLANT PROPERTIES ★★★★

**Shape and Size**
A climber with plenty of vigour. The stems that it produces are long and flexible. However, care is needed because the wood is more brittle than that of many other roses, and if you try to bend it too much it will snap. Growing to between 4.5 and 7.5m (15–25ft) tall and 2.4–4.5m (8–15ft) wide, this is a substantial climber.

**Position**
Somewhere with good light and some direct sunlight.

**Hardiness**
With protection it will be safe to try in cold areas.

### FOLIAGE PROPERTIES ★★★

**Colour**
Leaves are dark green and lustrous. It produces a good quantity of leaves low down, so there should be no problem with legginess.

**Health Check**
Look forward to a trouble-free experience. Any problems will be late in the season.

**Garden Uses**
In beds and borders or as an individual to make a splash.

### OVERALL ASSESSMENT ★★★★

✔ Simplicity and beauty of the flowers.
✖ Questionably hardy in cold positions; predilection towards downy mildew.

# *Morning Jewel*

## Climbing Rose (Climber)

   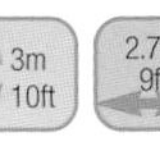 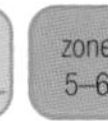

3m 10ft · 2.7m 9ft · zone 5–6

### FLOWER PROPERTIES ★★★

**Colour**

A very bright, almost shocking sugary pink, with a tiny white eye. It stands out from a distance and polarizes opinion – you either love it or hate it. It is impervious to the ravages of rain or excess sun, retaining almost all its colour until the petals fall.

**Size and Shape**

Plump buds open to produce flowers with about 20 petals. Blooms are wide – 8cm (3in) across – with the petals retaining a concave shape for most of the flower's life.

**Scent**

Best described as absent. This rose is for visual enjoyment.

**Production**

The first flush of flower in the summer is wonderful. Clustered in sets of five buds, the flowers open to cover the entire plant. All you see is a wall of colour: no leaf and no gaps. The repeat bloom is not as dense and can be improved by deadheading after the first flush.

### PLANT PROPERTIES ★★★★

**Shape and Size**

A climber that is restrained in its growth. It may be kept from 1.8–3m (6–10ft) tall and 1.5–2.7m (5–9ft ) wide. The plant generates enough canes to train into a good fan shape. The wood is stiff, so do not try to bend it too much when training it.

**Position**

Happy in either sun or shade, so any position is suitable.

**Hardiness**

This rose is a tough cookie. Worth trying in all areas.

### FOLIAGE PROPERTIES ★★★★★

**Colour**

Light to mid-green and very shiny. There is plenty of foliage, and it looks great behind the flowers in early summer.

**Health Check**

This rose has always had a good reputation for health, but in adverse conditions it can be afflicted by downy mildew.

**Garden Uses**

On walls, garden structures or fences. It will even perform well in north-facing sites with poor light.

### OVERALL ASSESSMENT 

✔ Hardiness and ability to perform in difficult positions.

✖ Requires deadheading for a good second flush.

# New Dawn

## Climbing Rose (Climber)

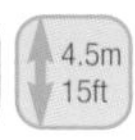

zone 6–7

### FLOWER PROPERTIES ★★★★★

**Colour**

Very gentle and restful: the most tender mother-of-pearl pink. In the bud the colour may be a little deeper, lightening as the bloom opens. There is a risk of damage from heavy rain.

**Size and Shape**

Flower structure is somewhat informal. The petals are a mixture of concave and convex – a success of random organization over structured symmetry. There are only 25 petals in each flower, which rarely exceeds 6cm (2.5in) in diameter.

**Scent**

Traditional rose scent – a wonderful wafting perfume from a plant in full flower on a warm summer evening.

**Production**

Clusters of five flowers are produced evenly over the plant, which means there is no shortage of blooms. The early flowering is better than that late in the season.

### PLANT PROPERTIES ★★★

**Shape and Size**

This is an enjoyable climber to grow. The canes are long and easy to train to the horizontal or vertical. Growing to a size that is controllable – between 2.7 and 4.5m (9–15ft) tall by 1.8 to 3m (6–10ft) wide – with plenty of growth to make a substantial framework to support the bloom, it has all the essential features of a climbing rose.

**Position**

Tolerant of aspects facing any four points of the compass, even in fairly shaded locations.

**Hardiness**

Although the flower may look delicate, the plant is robust and happy to tackle all but the most severely challenging environments.

### FOLIAGE PROPERTIES ★★★

**Colour**

There is an abundance of leaf, in a mid-green that works well with the flower colour.

**Health Check**

Generally a trouble-free rose. In adverse conditions blackspot or downy mildew may attack.

**Garden Uses**

On any structure in the garden, especially good for arches and pergolas.

### OVERALL ASSESSMENT ★★★★

✔ Unrivalled ability on arches and similar structures. Very pretty in bloom.

✖ It would be better with more foliage and an increased capacity to repel disease.

# Penny Lane

## Climbing Rose (Climber)

### FLOWER PROPERTIES ★★★★★

**Colour**

A delicate shade, often described as honey champagne. There is a little splash of pink in the early stages of the flower, but this later fades towards white.

**Size and Shape**

Round buds open to become large flowers, well endowed with petals, sometimes as many as 70. The flowers can reach 9cm (3.5in) in diameter, with large petals around the outside and smaller, shorter petals crammed into the centre. With all these petals, it is a long-lasting flower, able to withstand all but the heaviest rainstorms.

**Scent**

Individual blooms have a moderate scent with a musk base. *En masse* the blooms perfume the evening air.

**Production**

This has to be among the most productive climbers. It creates clusters of flower, often exceeding 11 buds each. The clusters open over a long period, and it produces a succession of clusters late into the season. There will be flowers for many weeks every season.

### PLANT PROPERTIES ★★★★★

**Shape and Size**

A very well-behaved climber. Growth is adequately strong for most uses, but not too vigorous, reaching between 2.7 and 4.3m (9–4ft) tall and 1.8–3m (6–10ft) wide. The canes are supple, which makes them easy to train on to most structures.

**Position**

Tolerant of a wide range of conditions and worth trying in all sites, even those with shade.

**Hardiness**

Hardiness is one of its virtues; with protection it will thrive in the coldest areas.

### FOLIAGE PROPERTIES ★★★★

**Colour**

Producing a veritable blanket of leaf along the stems, there will always be a contrasting background to the lightly coloured flowers. The leaves have a reassuring dark green colour and deep sheen.

**Health Check**

Able to withstand most ailments without too much problem. In some conditions powdery mildew may make an appearance late in the season.

**Garden Uses**

On any structure or vertical surface that requires covering.

### OVERALL ASSESSMENT ★★★★★

✔ The pleasure of a rose that will always perform well.

✖ The colour is too pale for some people.

# List of Suppliers

There are many excellent suppliers for rose plants, some serving just a local community, and others that ship nationwide or internationally. Here are some that are worth trying, but you should always be willing to try others, as new rose nurseries are regularly starting up.

Don't forget to search on the internet for more information on growers and suppliers. In addition to the suppliers listed here there are Garden Centers to visit. Good garden centers will provide strong and successful plants.

## USA AND CANADA

**Edmunds Roses**
6235 SW Kahle Road
Wilsonville, Oregon
USA 97070-9727
Tel: 888-481-7673
www.edmundsroses.com

**Heirloom Old Garden Roses**
24062 NE Riverside Drive
St. Paul, Oregon
USA 97137-9715
Tel: 503-538-1576 Fax:
www.heirloomroses.com

**Jackson & Perkins**
1 Rose Lane
Medford, Oregon
USA 97501
Tel: 1-877-322-2300
Fax: 1-800-242-0329
www.jackson-perkins.com

**Pickering Nurseries, Inc.**
670 Kingston Rd.
Pickering, Ontario
Canada L1V 1A6
Tel: 905-839-2111
Fax: 905-839-4807
www.pickeringnurseries.com

## UK

**R. Harkness & Co. Ltd**
Hitchin,
Herts. SG4 OJT
Tel: 01462 420402
E-mail: harkness@roses.co.uk
Web: www.roses.co.uk

**James Cocker & Sons**
Rose Specialists
Whitemyres,
Lang Stracht,
Aberdeen, Scotland
AB15 6XH
Tel. No. 01224 313261
Fax: No. 01224 312531
www.roses.uk.com

**C&K Jones**
Golden Fields Nursery,
Barrow Lane,
Tarvin, Cheshire
CH3

**Fryer's Roses**
Manchester Rd.
Knutsford, Cheshire
WA16 0SX
Tel: 44 01 565 755 455

## GERMANY

**Rosen Union**
61231 Bad Neuheim-Steinfurth
Steinfurther Hauptstrasse 25
Germany

**W. Kordes Sohne**
Rosenstrasse 54
Klein Offenseth
Sparrieshoop 25365
Germany

## Denmark

**Martin Jensens Planteskole**
Stavelsager 9
Skovby
5400 Bogense
Denmark

## HOLLAND

**Jan Timmermans VOF**
Rijksweg 42
6049 GW Herten
Holland

Roparu Rosen VOF
Ien de Nej Erf 32
5861 CG Wanssum
Holland
Tel: 31 478 532 841
Fax: 31 478 531 771

Fa. Jac Verschuren - Pechtold
Kalkhofseweg 6a
5443 NA Haps
Holland
www.verschuren-pechtold.nl

## BELGIUM

**Fa. Willem van Herreweghe**
Nieuwstraat 50
B-9260 Serskamp
Belgium
Tel: 32 093 690 176
Fax: 32 (0)93 661 957
www.willemvanherreweghe.be

## FRANCE

**Edirose**
RN6/Chesnes
38070 St Quentin Fallavier
France
Tel: 04 74 94 04 36
Fax: 04 74 95 54 16

## NEW ZEALAND

Matthews Nurseries Ltd
Wanganui
www.rosesnz.co.nz

# Index

Page numbers in italics indicate an illustration in the Choosing and Growing section, but note that all roses (listed under *Rosa*) have an illustration also.

# Acknowledgements

All photographs supplied by Steve Wooster except on the following pages.

29, 31 and 33 Holt Studios/Nigel Cattlin

21, 30, 44, 49, 63, 71, 79, 101, 102, 103, 108, 111, 115, 116, 119, 123, 124, 131, 138 Philip Harkness

# Zone Map of UK and Europe

A plant's winter hardiness is critical in deciding whether it is suitable for your garden. The map below divides the UK and Europe into 11 climactic zones based on average minimum temperatures. Find your zone and check the zone information in the plant directory to help you choose the plants most likely to flourish in your climate.

| | |
|---|---|
| **Zone 1** | Below -45°C (below -50°F) |
| **Zone 2** | -45° to -40°C (-50° to -40°F) |
| **Zone 3** | -40° to -34°C (-40° to -30°F) |
| **Zone 4** | -34° to -29°C (-30° to -20°F) |
| **Zone 5** | -29° to -23°C (-20° to -10°F) |
| **Zone 6** | -23° to -18°C (-10° to 0°F) |
| **Zone 7** | -18° to -15°C (0° to 10°F) |
| **Zone 8** | -15° to -12°C (10° to 20°F) |
| **Zone 9** | -12° to -6°C (20° to 30°F) |
| **Zone 10** | -6° to -1°C (30° to 40°F) |
| **Zone 11** | -1° to 5°C (above 40°F) |

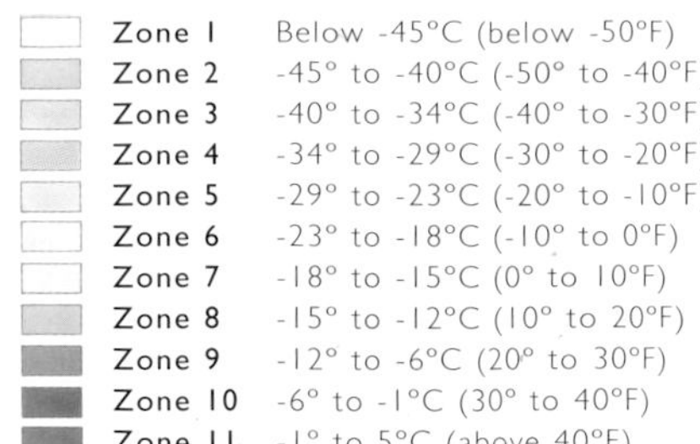

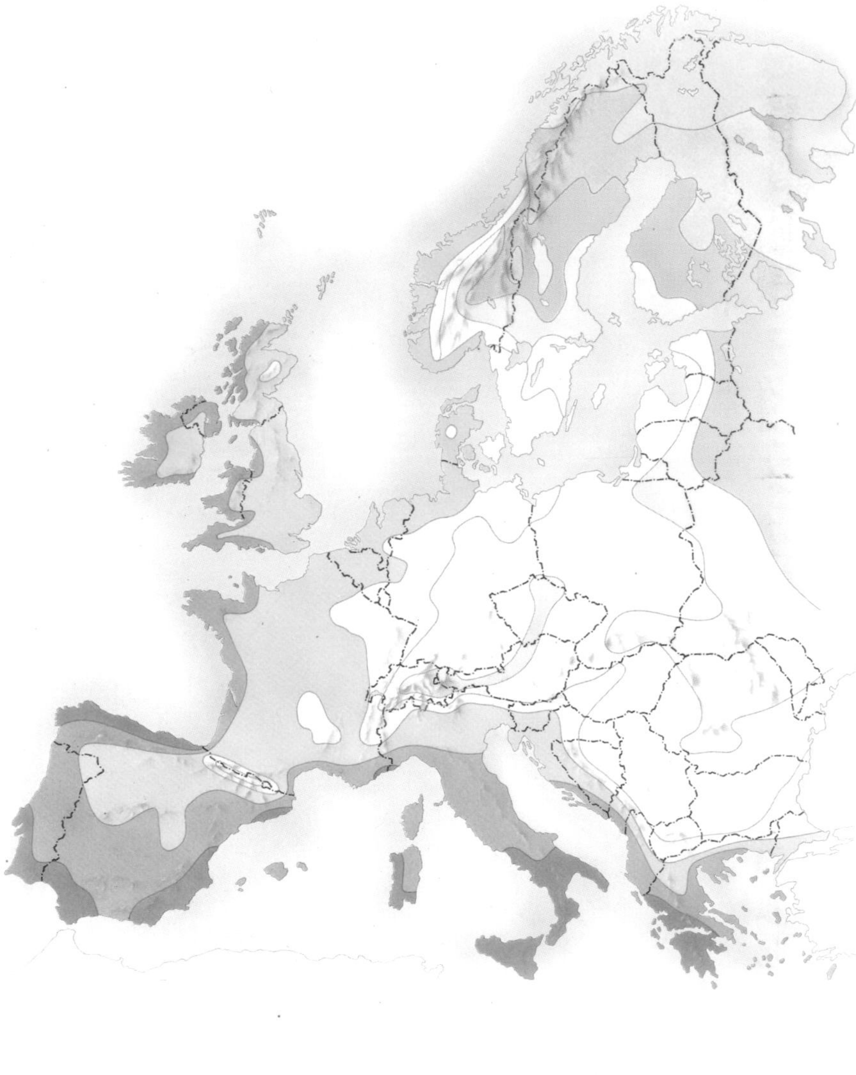